Maths in Context

A thematic approach

Deidre Edwards

Heinemann
Portsmouth, NH

HEINEMANN EDUCATIONAL BOOKS, INC.
361 Hanover Street Portsmouth, NH 03801
Offices and agents throughout the world

ISBN 0 435 08308 2

Published simultaneously in the United States
in 1990 by Heinemann
and in Australia by
Eleanor Curtain Publishing
906 Malvern Road
Armadale Vic 3046

Reprinted 1992

Production by Sylvana Scannapiego,
Island Graphics
Designed by Sarn Potter
Cover design by David Constable
Cover photograph by Northside Productions
Typeset by Trade Graphics Pty Ltd
Printed by SRM Production Services Sdn. Bhd., Malaysia

CONTENTS

◆

ACKNOWLEDGEMENTS

◆

I would like to express my thanks to all the teachers and children who have joined with me in discussing and trialling my ideas.

Thanks are also due to Peggy Giosis and John Flynn, whose encouragement was instrumental in helping me write this book.

PART ONE:

THE METHOD

1

WHY THEMATIC MATHS?

Why I started using a thematic approach

We are living in an increasingly technological world, and we need to prepare children to deal with change confidently, to seek a number of alternative solutions to a given situation, to evaluate these solutions and to share their ideas with others. Maths classes need to foster creative and divergent thinking rather than the idea that maths is about finding the 'right' answer.

Along with many other teachers, I found that in my language teaching an approach based on themes provided an interesting and often exciting learning environment in which new skills and concepts were immediately meaningful and relevant to the children. All aspects of language were related and the children's differing social and academic needs were catered for.

Working around themes, the children often developed their own areas of enquiry and learning. They were very interested in the theme and were eager to share their ideas, help each other and to offer suggestions.

The children enjoyed learning, learned faster and explored some aspects with surprising levels of complexity. They were also extremely highly motivated to want to learn more.

I became aware that many areas of mathematics were being mentioned constantly — during sharing time, during art activities and in particular during discussions centring on our current theme or topic.

The language the children used varied between ordinary day-to-day terms and mathematical language. During general discussions they included the language of number, space and measurement in problem-solving situations.

3

It became obvious that within our thematic studies it would be easy to incorporate mathematical ideas in 'real' problem-solving situations, and it seemed natural to try to extend the thematic approach to the teaching of maths.

Another area of concern to me has been the lack of thinking processes in maths teaching. Many of the situations presented in the maths lesson are perceived by the children (and some teachers too) to have only one method of solution and one answer.

I have taught children aged from five to twelve years in schools with a high percentage of students from non-English speaking families, usually with a very limited vocabulary. It was often assumed in these schools that children would have less difficulty with maths — implying that language was not relevant in maths. Indeed many of the children's answers were correct, but when questioned about their work, the thinking processes involved, why and when they would use the methods employed, the children would often reply, 'This is what you do during a maths lesson'. They did not relate what they were doing to maths in the real world; nor did they think to apply their own way of working to the problems. I attributed their replies and lack of explanation, in part, to a language problem, and so spent many hours relating language activities to mathematical concepts.

After transferring to a school where the children's language skills were well developed, I was amazed to encounter the same initial response: 'That's how you do it. My answer's right, isn't it?' It seemed that if the answer was right the teacher should not confuse matters by asking when and how this knowledge would be used!
Given

$$\begin{array}{r} 23 \\ \times 5 \\ \hline \end{array}$$

the children would complete it by saying:
'Three times five equals fifteen.
Put down the five and carry the one.'

$$\begin{array}{r} {}^{1}23 \\ \times 5 \\ \hline 5 \end{array}$$

When asked 'Why?' they replied, 'Because that's what you do when it's 15'.

In situations like this we need to ask 'Why?' again, to determine the extent of the child's understanding of place value and how it works, rather than accept a correct answer as an indication of understanding.

The following errors need to be questioned in the same way:
'How did you get your answer?'
'Why did you...?'
so that the misunderstanding can be identified and worked on.

$$\begin{array}{r} 23 \\ {}_5\times5 \\ \hline 151 \end{array}$$

What is 15?

$$\begin{array}{r} 23 \\ {}_1\times5 \\ \hline 105 \end{array}$$

What did the 1 being carried mean?

When presenting the same problem as a story to the children I found two contrasting responses. Either they did not recognise it as a 'mathematical' problem and so found the solution using their own strategies, or, seeing no immediate and familiar pattern, 'gave up'.

Everyone in our class is so excited. We are making biscuits to sell at the school fete. Yum. They smell delicious! We have decided that each of us will have enough mixture to make five big biscuits. How many will that make altogether?

Some children quickly jotted down

$$\begin{array}{r} 23 \\ \times5 \end{array}$$

Many knew that 5 times 20 was 100, then in a variety of ways approached 5 times 3. These included:
- counting on, 3 6 9 12 15
- using known number facts, 3 × 3 = 9, then counting on, 12 15, or 5 + 5 = 10 and 5 more make 15
- reversing 5 × 3 to 3 × 5, counting in fives, or using the known fact 5 × 3 = 15.

The 15 was then added to the 100, but interesting problems arose as to how the answer should be written — 10015 or 115?

Most of the above was accomplished confidently through mental computation, and often by children who had previously been unsuccessful with the written algorithm originally presented.

This example of interpreting story problems showed quite clearly that more variety in the presentation of maths lessons was essential to *all* children so that they could use mathematical language and devise their own strategies for solving problems.

The benefits of thematic maths

Maths becomes part of real life

When working on thematic maths sessions, mathematics can be seen to be part of our 'real life' situations. Mathematics need no longer be daily counting drill and the revision of algorithms, with perhaps the once-a-week measurement activity session.

The measurement activity session is one of the best aspects of mathematical teaching from which to begin planning your own thematic approach. Measurement activities can be developed to form the basis of many other class activities, and integrated with other mathematical and curriculum areas.

For example, following a visit to the zoo, one of the areas to be discussed could be the range of environments established for the animals: types and density of trees, rocks, water supply and area needed for each animal.

This could lead to further investigation of tree classification: tall, short, bushy; shade areas; thick and thin leaf cover; or to quantity of water — drinking water only; swimming pools for the birds, crocodiles, seals, bears.

Discussion and exploration are centred around something the children have seen and experienced at first hand so that they can identify the need for the estimations and calculations they are making.

Integration of mathematical language

Mathematical language is being developed together with ordinary language. For example, the tallest trees had the most sunlight, they overshadowed the smaller trees, blocking out most of the sun's stronger rays during the day.

Without being aware of it, we are thinking, exploring and using aspects of maths from the moment we first wake in the morning: 'What's the time? Is there enough hot water for my shower? How many sandwiches do I want for lunch today? Have I enough money to go shopping?' By taking a thematic approach we can provide situations in which the children can use maths naturally and spontaneously, perceiving a relevance and purpose to their work.

Traditional approaches to measurement present set areas to be measured, or measurements for children to record. By presenting a problem for the children to solve themselves, measurement tasks become a step on the way to solving the problem. The approaches the children make and use in their problem solving will be more challenging and relevant than those posed by teachers or most text books. Also, the use of problem solving and open-ended questions allows for alternative solutions, creativity and the development of divergent thinking skills, aspects not frequently found in the maths lesson. Following the zoo trip, problem-solving activities could include considerations of the enclosures, such as height, length, area, interior/exterior design, spatial awareness and construction (wall/fence type).

Using a thematic approach for mathematic development allows for the presentation of many similar problems ranging over a variety of experiences. Children may attempt one, several or all of these problems, depending on their ability and their interest. A wide range of different experiences enables them to initiate, consolidate and extend their own experiences, giving them some responsibility in their own learning. Some may need verbal support or guidance from their peer group or teacher, while others may choose to work independently, either individually or in groups.

Children share responsibility for learning

Allowing children freedom to explore problems themselves and to work independently gives the teacher additional freedom and time to interact with the children more effectively, to pose further thought-provoking questions, to observe and listen to the processes being utilised in the problem-solving issues and to evaluate each child's progress. The children will seek the teacher's assistance and knowledge when they need guidance in presenting or representing their work.

The responsibility of finding the most suitable processes, concrete equipment and recording materials is handed over to the children. The resulting sense of ownership provides motivation to continue, satisfaction with a successful solution and above all a positive view of maths which will be seen as useful and enjoyable. In this relaxed and more encouraging classroom atmosphere the activities will lead naturally to the discussion of the problem in hand.

The attentive teacher will be able not only to evaluate the children's strengths and weaknesses, but also to capitalise on their interests and suggestions in planning, consolidation, revision and extension activities.

Children gain confidence in their own abilities

Using the children's own suggestions shows them that we, as adults, value their thoughts and ideas. They gain confidence in their own and other children's abilities and with this confidence comes a far wider range of ideas, thoughts and questions and divergent thinking skills.

Children's individual differences are recognised and used to enhance the quality of learning. If a child's answer is 'different' from others it is essential to explore why it is different. Differences can arise from factors such as an oversight of one area, a computational or recording inaccuracy, the incorrect use of a process, misinterpretation of the question, or from two or more valid interpretations or solutions of the one problem. The suggestions made by the children show their depth of knowledge and perceptions of possible extension areas.

In this way there is no feeling of failure. No child is 'wrong'; rather there is the challenge to see if the solutions can be arrived at. Often the child labelled as an under-achiever has been rushed, not given sufficient time to think through the situation or problem and so an incorrect answer is given. The answer may well prove, upon further clarification, to be just one step short of the correct one. These children, when provided with security and additional time, not only reach the 'correct' answer but may also demonstrate that they have considered a number of different possibilities, adding their own creative thinking to the problem. Given such freedom and time, as well as teacher support, they can elucidate their ideas. This often provides stimulus for further activities in the same or different areas.

Conversely, children who are usually among the first to provide the correct answer will not feel the pressure of being expected to be correct at all times — or thinking all their answers are correct. They too will have time to contemplate other possible means of achieving the same answer, or a possible alternative answer.

The children will learn to respect and consider all answers, not only those of the few. Additional 'wait time' also enables these children to reconsider their results, how they achieved them, and avenues for further exploration. Again, this provides a fund of material from which the teacher can draw.

Different areas of the curriculum may be integrated

The thematic activities suggested during discussions will not always be mathematically based, but they should be accepted as part of the overall theme because there will always be an overlap of subject areas, an ongoing flow and inter-relationship between all areas. This reinforces the links between maths and the other curriculum areas. We cannot divorce maths from science, art, physical education or music; nor do we want to.

Summary

In summary, when children are presented with a challenge in the form of a theme which interests them they work for long periods of time seeking a variety of solutions. They question, argue and extend each other, explaining and elucidating their viewpoints to their peers and to themselves, time and again. They reinforce or order concepts they have learnt or believe. Sometimes they are forced to discard previous ideas in the light of a new development or to reassess their methods.

2

INTRODUCING THEMATIC
MATHS INTO THE CLASSROOM

Discussing/brainstorming

Share and discuss your ideas for a new approach with the children. If the concept is totally new to all of you, you may spend several sessions in discussion of issues such as the need for co-operation, for the sharing of ideas, the value of questioning and accepting responsibility for one's own materials and equipment. Most importantly, each child needs to be encouraged to accept the final goal of being responsible for his or her own learning. This will help establish a classroom atmosphere conducive to an open approach to mathematical education.

When planning your theme discuss the possible avenues that could be followed. Ask the children to help you plan and try new ideas. Ask them to consider ways in which they could, or would like to, develop the theme. Their suggestions may cover many curriculum areas, such as literature, art, mathematics, science or social education. Encourage the presentation of all ideas, as sometimes the one with the least apparent merit, with further input will develop to be the best. It must be made clear that these are suggestions from which several will be chosen.

Working with the whole class

In the initial stages it is often helpful to select one activity and work with the children as a whole class. This will enable experimentation in sharing ideas, discarding activities which may be inappropriate and finding or selecting a number of similar activities to cater for individual differences.

One of the following activities could be developed within the context of your chosen theme.

◆

Build a story

Using a variety of manipulative equipment the children could build their interpretation of the theme, either collectively or individually. One or several may then be selected to be explored in greater depth.

Adam and Ben had built the walls of their house. They found they could not get the top or the bottom perfectly even when the sides all had the same number of blocks. They found

$$4 \times 6 = 24 \qquad \text{build 2 more}$$
$$2 \times 6 + 2 \times 7 \ = 26 \qquad \text{build 2 more}$$
$$4 \times 7 = 28$$

As they continued they found the relationship between the two and four times tables.

Ben is trying to work out how to place these blocks to make an angled roof. After experimenting he and Adam built a flat roof and then used the blocks behind for covering. The next day we used Timberblock and built a cubby house with a roof for our room.

Kate and Olivia built their house and their main concern was to have sliding doors from room to room. Through trial and error they discovered that the blocks needed room for extension and preferably were of an even height. At this stage of their development they really weren't concerned with opposite walls being the same length!

These blocks are a challenge to all ages. I was at first surprised by the sustained interest shown by older children, until I found myself equally keen to 'add a bit'.

Kristy, Nick and Belinda are trying to keep their house structure balanced.

'It's the same height, why won't it stand?'

'Put this bit on top. Whoops!'

'It needs more added on the side to hold it up.'

They then found that some of the rods were not pushed right in and the extra circle added in the middle, while it balanced initially, upset the balance when the height became greater. They were also seeking a pleasing visual effect.

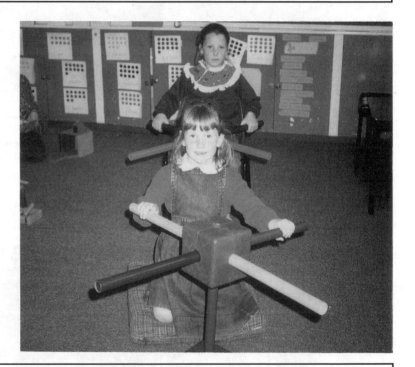

Kristy and Georgia made steering wheels to drive away to get some more building materials.

These blocks are excellent when studying angles, rotation, degrees and the points of the compass.

Write a story

Together write an imaginative wall story or book to develop ordinary and mathematical language.

EXAMPLE

The children had made butterflies using wire and cellophane. When we hung them up in the classroom we discussed the number of butterflies, their corresponding patterns, which colour had been chosen most often, the butterflies with similar wings, their position in relation to each other, etc.

Suddenly the sunlight shone through the window and we found the yellow butterflies were harder to see. We discussed the word 'camouflage.' Our wall story developed spontaneously from the ensuing discussion.

Our butterflies were out in the warm, bright sun. But we couldn't see the yellow ones. They were camouflaged sitting on the yellow flowers. $\boxed{24 - 8 = 16}$ We counted and only saw sixteen.

Half of the purple butterflies flew way, way up and vanished from sight. $\boxed{\begin{array}{l} 8 - 4 = 4 \\ \frac{1}{2} \text{ of } 8 = 4 \end{array}}$ $\boxed{\begin{array}{l} 16 - 4 = 12 \\ \text{I can only see 12.} \end{array}}$

Soon the red butterfly flew away. He wanted to find some other butterflies who were the same colour. $\boxed{12 - 1 = 11}$

Suddenly — a big, floppy puppy came racing through the flowers and the yellow butterflies swirled up. We could see them again. $\boxed{11 + 8 = 19}$ Butterflies everywhere!

Oh dear! Here comes a flock of birds. We think they'll gobble them up for dinner. $\boxed{19 - 19 = 0}$

Thank goodness! Here comes a big, fat cat ready for a bird feast. The butterflies were safe. $\boxed{\begin{array}{l} 0 + 19 = 19 \\ \text{They escaped being eaten.} \end{array}}$

We hope by tomorrow all our butterflies are back.

How many would need to come back? $\boxed{19 + \square = 24}$

We'd love to have twice as many butterflies in our garden.

$\boxed{24 \times 2 = 48}$ $\boxed{\begin{array}{l} \text{Twice as many yellow butterflies} \\ 8 + 8 = 16 \qquad 2 \times 8 = 16 \end{array}}$

$\boxed{\begin{array}{l} \text{Twice as many pink butterflies} \\ 7 + 7 = 14 \qquad 2 \times 7 = 14 \end{array}}$ $\boxed{\begin{array}{l} \text{twice as many cats} \\ 2 \times 1 = 2 \qquad 1 + 1 = 2 \end{array}}$

What about three times as many?

Solve a problem

Use a real life situation from the theme to set a problem-solving task. From the theme of pets or shopping, for example, you could try the following problem or a similar one.

My puppy Tyson is growing very big. We play chasey together and I've just taught him to race after the ball, then bring it back to me. It's great fun!

> If I stand at the path it's 27 metres to the back fence. After eight turns he's usually puffed out so we stop and I give him a drink. On Sunday he only had six turns — then he chased the cat to the back fence and wouldn't come back.
> How far does he chase the ball each week?
> How far did he chase it last week?

But Mum says he's really best at eating!
He eats a whole 1.2 kilogram can of food every morning.
Henry, our other dog, only eats half a can.
At night they both eat dry food.
Mum buys a 5 kilogram bag of Meaty Bites and a 2 kilogram bag of Good-O each week.

> How many cans does Mum buy each week?
> How much would they weigh?
> Could you lift that weight?
> What else is as heavy?
> How much dry food do the dogs eat at each meal?

Some of the questions are straightforward. Others could have a variety of answers depending on the children's interpretation of the story. For example, does Henry eat as much dry food as Tyson, or only half as much?

Working with groups or individuals

As the children become familiar with this approach they will be able to pursue, in groups or independently, many of the other suggestions made during the brainstorming session/s.

Children who have been working in a more formal or traditional manner may require guidance in aspects of working co-operatively and flexibly. For example, the need to consider all solutions; to look for solutions that will provide the best explanation, the least amount of computation, or the best range of recording activities.

As well as allowing the children to experience 'wait time', the teacher should take time to consider appropriate responses and questions. Try to ask questions that encourage the children to take risks, look for alternative methods, push themselves further, but at the same time demonstrate how positively you feel towards their responses.

Give support

While it is important to provide support and structure and ensure that the mathematics is at the children's level of competence, it is also important to allow and encourage the children freedom of thought and activity, for the teacher to be recognised as a participant rather than the initiator of all mathematical activity. It is equally important not to give so much freedom that the children's ideas become lost in a sea of confusion and inappropriate 'busy' activities.

The teacher needs to be aware of the children's progress and to act as a catalyst when required. The children will initially need the teacher's support frequently, but the need will lessen as confidence in their own ability develops. Support may again be sought when the children are working in a new or unknown area, so expect this. Also, with this discovery approach to mathematical learning, a much wider range of concepts and processes will be attempted and used by the children at one time. In an activity such as making fruit salad for lunch most areas of measurement, space and computational skills could be involved.

So be fully aware of the developmental steps of learning in each of the mathematical areas and don't be surprised if the children appear to 'leap over' or 'slide back' in new situations.

Support may be in the form of verbal comments, asking the child to show the class or another child his or her work, suggesting another familiar method or piece of alternative equipment that may be more appropriate; helping the child to verbalise the problem before commencing, or stopping midway to clarify work already completed; or even suggesting that everything has become muddled.

'Let's have another try.'

'Let's just leave it. Tomorrow we'll try again.'

'Would you like some help there?'

'Let's stick at it. We've nearly got it!'

'I'm a little confused. Can you show me again?'

'Hey. That's really great. Can you show us how you worked out the problem?'

Opportunities for feedback

Given the opportunity, children will readily tell you of their successes and/or difficulties. Partial success in a task should also be recognised positively. Learning will flourish in a happy, relaxed classroom atmosphere.

Communicating during a mathematical activity with a most competent seven year old emphasised this for me.

During our preliminary discussion Nicholas had been highly motivated to solve the problem being presented and had suggested several ways he could attempt this. To my surprise, when he began work he became quite confused, although he was using materials with which he was very familiar and employing mathematical language, concepts and processes he had previously used most effectively. Realising his own confusion, he replaced his concrete materials in their containers. He then started the activity anew.

Prior to this the children had acquired a number of badges printed with 'I Love Maths', 'Supermaths', etc. They often wore them when they felt they really deserved praise, or most importantly, felt pleased with their own achievement or performance.

Having persevered for quite a long time, Nicholas swept the materials into their containers, and with a sigh and a grin said, 'I think I need a cotton wool badge. That's what my brain's like. I'll have another go tomorrow.'

The next day he completed the task within a few minutes. In the intervening time he had successfully completed a variety of language, science and music based tasks.

Would the result have been the same if Nicholas had had to continue his work until it was correct?

Observe and take notes

To maximise the effectiveness of your teaching it is necessary to really listen to and observe the children as they work at their activities and tasks.

Your observations, both formal and informal, are important. Anecdotal notes made during an activity are useful for:

- later reference during individual progress reporting and evaluation
- planning of lessons to cover all facets of the mathematics curriculum
- evaluating the effectiveness of the task in meeting its aim.

Remember that areas of possible confusion to a child may be better resolved by an explanation from another child who was successful than by a further explanation by the teacher.

Ask questions and listen

I have become aware of the need for a varied range of questioning techniques. Sometimes an exact or specific answer is necessary, in which case closed questions are essential, as in most other maths lessons. More often, though, questions need to be open-ended to allow for varied approaches and responses.

EXAMPLE

'How many frogs could this pond hold?'

This question allowed the children to establish their own range, complexity and method of approach. It also provided me with an ideal situation in which to observe the children's mathematical thinking.

They responded by being the frogs and moving the tables so that most of·the classroom became the pond. They initially assumed the normal frog crouch, placing themselves side by side, but when they ran out of 'frogs' the children from the back came forward. Several instigated this move themselves; others were reticent because they had already been counted.

The comments made by the children at this stage gave me insights into their mathematical development:

'But then we wouldn't have room to land when we jumped', said Kim.

'What if we wanted to swim?' asked Jodie.

Further investigation was encouraged by not providing any solutions but countering with more questions.

'Well... how much space would a frog need?

Does he only need room to swim?'

From the original question a whole range of mathematical questions developed as the children went on to discuss various body movements, the space taken by frogs and other animals, obstacles in the water, e.g. rocks and weeds, the volume of water and variation of the depth, the perimeter of the pond and many other variables. What if it rained, or there was a period of drought?

In this way children can develop the ability to ask questions. Furthermore, the questions are really discriminating and open-ended.

From their initial conversations I was able to encourage the children to follow through the more pertinent questions they had posed, which involved mathematical discovery and learning.

At first I took responsibility for leading to a worthwhile area of study. Of the ideas, some were more valuable than others, some needed elucidation, others might have been fun but were merely repetitious. While I did encourage repetition of activities through a variety of situations to consolidate the children's understanding, I also tried to ensure that they had the opportunity, within the activities, not only to consolidate but to refine and build on their current knowledge.

Children telling you what they know

Adam described the shopping spree he had had with his family. He told me that he had wanted a new skateboard but it was too expensive. He had only a $10 note and two $5s. However, after he'd received the $20 his grandmother had promised for his birthday the following week, in five weeks he would be able to buy the skateboard.

Why the five weeks wait?

He had previously calculated that he also needed his $2 a week pocket money. The skateboard cost $49 and six year old Adam realised he would have change — later in the day he told me it would be $1. Other children joined in Adam's skateboard discussion. There was a constant change from everyday language to mathematical language to mathematical symbolism as Adam and the children clarified the problem.

Adam: 'I have $20. It isn't enough.'

Belinda: 'Do you have a $20 note?'

Adam: 'No. I have a $10 and a $5 and a $5'.

Nick: 'That's two fives are ten plus ten equals twenty. He's right. We can write it like this: $2 \times 5 + 10 = 20$'

(I had encouraged the children to check each other's findings. When I felt they were confidently discussing particular concepts, e.g. addition, multiplication, etc., I would often jot down our findings or numbers we needed to remember. The children were keen to do this for me and consequently for themselves.)

Belinda: 'How much more do you need?'

Adam: 'Well, the whole skateboard is $49.'

(Adam had not really worked out the exact difference. At home he had kept adding his money until he reached the desired amount. However he did realise that the older children could work it out for themselves if he gave them the price.)

Nathan: 'Hmm. $20 and $20 make $40 — so he needs $29.'

At this stage, to assist the younger children, who were most interested but starting to feel puzzled by the rush of explanations, I asked Nathan (7 years) to show the class how he had arrived at his answer. Using counters that were close to hand as dollar units he showed us.

□ □ □
□ □ □ □
□ □ □ □
□ □ □ □
□ □ □ □ □
        20

'Then I had to get to $49.

I know 20 + 20 = 40'

I asked him to place them out, then we all checked.

□ □ □
□ □ □ □
□ □ □ □
□ □ □ □   □ □ □ □ □ □ □ □ □
□ □ □ □ □   □ □ □ □ □ □ □ □ □
      20   21, 22, 23, 24, ...40

'Then I knew I needed 9 more.

That's 40. (He indicated the blocks.)

□ □ □ □ □ □ □ □ □

Then it's 41   42   43   44...49. See!'

He placed out the blocks as he counted.

Leah: 'Yes. Look. That's $49 he needs.' (She indicated the blocks with her hand.)

Next she covered one group of twenty with her hand.

'He's got that much so 49 – 20 = 29' (She wrote this on a card.)

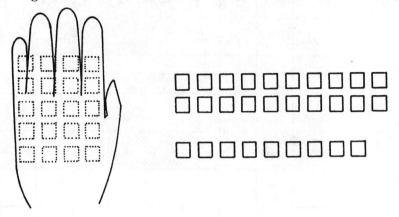

'Will Adam really be able to get his skateboard in five weeks time?'

In response to this question the children used a wide variety of aids and strategies, each of which told a lot about what they knew and could do. These included using fingers, counters, play money, bead frames, calendars and recording in a number of ways. Some children

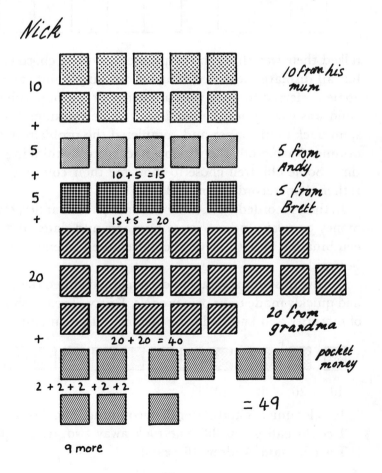

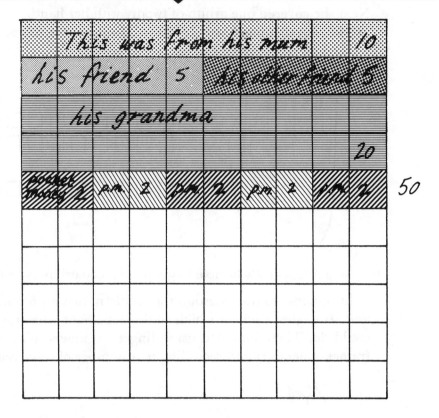

talked their way through the problem. Others chose to work quietly, but all displayed a varied range of working habits and mannerisms. Some preferred to work with a partner or a group, others alone. One child was gazing out the window. Was he working? Yes. Suddenly he spun back to his paper and completed the problem in the minimum of time. Gazing out the window had been his thinking and planning time. Some children chose to show me their counters or play money rather than record their work.

In their recorded work some children pasted circles, etc. to represent money or weeks; others wrote numbers and dates and some wrote a combination of both. Several children used calendar sheets and number grids.

During this time several children had recounted the blocks and some had quickly made their own models. Kristy (7 years) showed her depth of maturity and knowledge by placing out green and yellow counters.

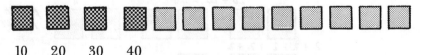

10   20   30   40

'It's a lot quicker and easier than counting.' She thought for a minute.
'I could call green 20'. She took away two green squares.
'I get it', said Andrew (6 years).

20

Kristy wrote,

June				
SUNDAY	4	11	18	25
MONDAY	5	QUEEN'S BIRTHDAY (NOT WA) 12	19	26
TUESDAY	6	13	20	27
WEDNESDAY Adams birthday	7 $10	14	21	28
THURSDAY 1	8	15	22	29
FRIDAY 2	9	from Grandma 16 ↓	23	30
SATURDAY 3	Party $5 +$5 10	$20 17	+2 =42 24	

July				
SUNDAY 30	2	9	16	23
MONDAY 31	3	10	17	24
TUESDAY	4	11	18	25
WEDNESDAY	5	12	19	26
THURSDAY	6	13	20	27
FRIDAY	7	14	21	28
SATURDAY +2 1=44	+2 8=46	+2 15=48	+2 22=50	29

Adam will have
$1 left over.
He'll probably buy lollies - or save it.

Some children recorded their findings by using coloured paper squares for the notes ($20, $10, $5) and coin stamps for the $2 and $1. They decided not to use smaller denominations of coins as we'd get 'millions of answers'. They were aware of the possibilities of using other coins.

Some children were interested to know the actual date when Adam would get his skateboard. We followed this up later in the week, using the class calendar or individual ones. We also wrote imaginary stories about Adam earning extra money on particular days or being 'naughty' and not receiving his full amount of pocket money each week, and wrote equations alongside to clarify this. Others wrote creative stories describing how Adam felt prior to and when he actually bought his skateboard. They were most expressive. Language and mathematics were hand in hand.

Contrast this activity and the information I gained about each child's understanding with what might have happened if I had asked the children to solve

$$10 + 2 \times 5 + 20 + 5 \times 2$$

A correct answer would possibly have been arrived at by several of the children, but to what purpose? It would have had no relevance for them and would have given me very little insight into how they were thinking and what they actually knew.

Integrating thematic maths into the wider curriculum

Using a thematic approach to mathematics should not imply that all aspects of maths must be related to the current theme. Select those activities and areas that are meaningful to the children and can be worked through spontaneously, then move to the next appropriate activity. Some themes may last several weeks, others days or only hours.

Occasionally there may be an aspect of maths that you feel cannot be incorporated into, or arise naturally from, your thematic work, but is important for the children to learn. If you present this aspect to the children it may well be that their working conversation will lead to a 'real life' situation that can be explored.

There should be a balance between the variety of thematic maths activities and activities arising spontaneously from other situations such as free play with manipulative equipment, 'morning talk', media news events, etc. and those which may be ongoing, such as recording special events or marking off the days on the calendar.

Birthdays

Birthdays are special. Most children look forward to bringing a large cake, small cakes or something special to school on their birthday.

The children in my class now eagerly mark off the days until our next 'Birthday maths'.

22

'Blowing out candles is fun!'

'How many ways can you blow out seven candles?'

The latter question came from Mark when we had two children turning seven and one turning six...and the cakes arrived together!

He had observed that the first seven year old had blown out two candles, then five, using two breaths. The next child had blown out four candles, then none, then three. The six year old didn't have as many to blow out. Mark recorded his observations and the class went on to discover further possibilities:

$$2 + 5 = 7$$
$$4 + 0 + 3 = 7$$
$$7 - 1 = 6$$
$$6 + 1 = 7$$

Other related problems were then posed.

- How many Smarties were needed to decorate 26 cakes with 5 Smarties each?
  (See Party Time.)
- Which cake is the biggest?
- Does each packet of Smarties have the same number and colours?

This became a follow-up activity at home, involving other family members.

We now write a maths story or discuss a problem-solving activity then record our observations for each birthday as it arises. The 'Birthday maths' is displayed for the day and *always* taken home. Parents are just as keen as the children to share this experience. Their expectant look and the children's chatter and explanations as they meet at the end of the day clearly spell success.

Developing themes into maths stories

The children and I often write as a group or individually about our day-to-day activities, excursions, special events or new information we acquired. Gradually we have included mathematical themes.

Shark story

A huge shark caught at Phillip Island was front-page news in the daily papers.

In response to the newspaper story the children went on to create their own maths stories. They used concrete materials to build and act them out. The stories were often recorded and displayed for others to read and the number concepts embedded in them were recorded in what the children decided was 'like shorthand or writing initials for someone's name', either before or after the actual longhand story. This reinforced the relationship between the mathematical symbols and the more informal, natural language of the stories.

> The shark saw six fish swimming along.
> He thought he'd have them for his dinner. Snap! Yum! He ate four of the fish. Two lucky fish stayed hiding in the weeds away from the shark for a long, long time.
> Story + maths $6 - 4 = 2$

As we progressed sometimes we started with the story then recorded the equation; sometimes we started with the equation and created our own story.

Often a group or class story was changed due to later input.

> Another shark came along from the opposite direction and ate the two fish who were hiding in the weeds.
> $$6 - 4 - 2 = 0$$

> When the shark gobbled up the two fish he also swallowed five big pieces of seaweed.
> $$2 + 5 = 7$$
> That's seven things the shark ate in one gulp.

Developing maths stories into books

As our stories progressed we found we were making maths books. Each page added to the events and thus changed the equation. We developed many concepts along the same lines.

Maths stories have become an integral part of our theme-based mathematics programme. I discovered that stories may be written at the beginning of a theme, generating interest in an area the teacher feels is needed. For example:

- an area not previously covered
- an extension or challenge to current understanding
- related problem-solving activities
- involving individual children more by including their names in the stories.

After I had posed some problems as stories the children began writing their own problem stories.

> On the way to the shop Kristy lost 20c of her milk money. Her friends gave her the change they had in their pockets. Would it be enough?

As in the example above, the problems are often not entirely clear.

In this case the children are invited to decide how many friends Kristy had and how much money they each had. In real life many problems are not clearly defined or do not have one right answer, so it is a valuable experience for the children to meet problems of this type.

Stories can also be written to describe a series of events, as in the examples that follow. These can become wall stories or books. The recording can be organised in such a way that the creative story is written alongside the number story, or they can be kept separate so that some time later the children can try to find the equation to suit the story.

This is how one such story developed.

> Nathan had 2c and 5c in his pocket. Can you make up an interesting story about this?

The children responded with:

> Nathan put his hands in his jeans' pocket. Ah! 2c. Hmm! He thought he had more than that. As he wriggled around he found another 5c caught right down in the corner of his pocket.
> $$2c + 5c = 7c$$

> Belinda searched the ground.
> 'Here's some!' she called out. 'This 5c rolled into the gutter. And I've got 4c left in my bag from my lunch order.'
> $$5c + 4c = 9c$$

> Nathan and Belinda gave their coins to Kristy.
> $$7c + 9c = 16c$$

Other algorithms can be developed for further recording.

$$2\times5c + 3\times2c$$
$$2\times5c + 2\times1c + 2\times2c, \text{ etc.}$$

The story can be continued as Kristy counts all her money and buys the milk. She may share it with her friends. Will Mum need some for cooking, or breakfast?

Developing themes from literature

Many children's books are suitable for mathematical exploration and development. The story provides a structure for developing number, space and measurement concepts and can be retold in the children's words, or recorded mathematically. After reading part of the story the children can be invited to predict:

What if...?

What might happen?

and so will explore a wide range of possibilities.

I have enjoyed using *The Doorbell Rang* by Pat Hutchins with children of all ages. The children discussed and developed the story, using mathematical concepts and language that matched their ability levels. Follow-on activities have ranged from counting biscuits to making, costing and selling them for a fund-raising stall.

In *The Doorbell Rang* Ma has baked a plate of cookies for her two children to share. As more and more visitors arrive the cookies need to be shared again and again.

I have used the following techniques successfully with this book.

1 Using the story structure for combined drama-maths activities.

2 Introducing new possibilities:

What if some biscuits were bigger?

Would the cat in the picture have got one?

What happened when he was alone on the table with the cookies?

3 Writing sequels or alternatives based on the story structure:

What happened when Mum baked the cookies?

Why did she only have one tray?

Did she save one tray, give it away, burn some?

4 Reversing the approach by providing an equation and building, modelling or writing a story about it. This can range from one or two sentences to a complete story covering explanations, possible side-tracking or posing further questions at a more advanced level.

When working from literature I have found that ensuing discussion provides a wealth of activities beyond the scope of the actual book being used. However it is not possible to do everything that's thought of — being selective is essential to prevent a book from being ruined by 'overkill'.

With so many ideas coming forward at once I've found it helpful to look for a sequence or a number pattern to use as a guide. In all thematic work, seeking a pattern is a good idea.

As they write their stories the children also develop an understanding of the need for sequencing and pattern in both their story writing and their mathematical computations.

Sharing ideas with colleagues

As the children need support, so does the teacher. Much of your support will come from the enjoyment and satisfaction you gain from working with the children on the maths theme and from their evident overall development. They will delight in their ability to use their mathematical skills in specific and incidental situations.

Encouragement and support will also come from other members of your teaching staff. Discuss what you are planning, how you are going about it, and ask others to share this with you. You may choose to share the same theme with another class. For example, when visiting the zoo or the traffic school you could plan together or separately, then share your ideas. This can be at the same grade level, but need not be so. Sharing and making comparisons can be equally effective at any level.

You can also share ideas on approach, questioning techniques, or be a catalyst for different ideas on the same or different themes.

You could consider:

- how you felt during the activities
- whether you covered the areas you set out to cover
- indications for future areas to pursue
- difficulties that arose and whether they were due to lack of understanding or explanation, uncertainty of approach, trying too much too soon — or not enough. Were difficulties only those that should be expected when we try a new approach?

However, don't become so analytical that you develop a negative rather than a positive attitude. Be confident. Share your successes and build upon these. As you share and discuss your ideas you will be clarifying and ordering them for yourself.

Just as you expect individual differences between your children, expect them between your colleagues too.

A number of classes in which I assisted — with children ranging in age from five to ten years — had been exploring the themes of dinosaurs and dragons through language. The children and teachers were most enthusiastic to incorporate areas of maths into these programmes. Several found they had in fact been using mathematical language, concepts and skills. They quickly and most effectively explored the potential of such activities further. While there were many similarities between the grades in the problems being explored, in the stories related, the games developed, etc., there was an ever-widening range of activities developing, due to the children's ages and to class and individual interests and abilities.

Three teachers introduced an identical activity to their classes. Each came back to report on very successful but very different areas of maths being covered. This divergence of approaches and ideas is also most evident if an activity is presented to a class and the children work independently or in groups, rather than as a class.

Ideas should be shared. You may like to try someone else's idea or theme, but don't extend activities to the point of saturation.

3
ASSESSING MATHS IN
A THEMATIC ACTIVITY

While working with children you will automatically be assessing many varied and important learning outcomes. The strengths and weaknesses of each child's progress, both in knowledge and learning strategies, should be clear to both you and the student and be readily discussed to provide the basis for further exploration.

Formal mathematical testing will usually confirm the assessment you have already formed of the child's performance in maths. In *The Mathematics Curriculum and Teaching Program — Assessment Alternatives in Mathematics,* David Clarke states that 'formal assessment using tests commonly does little more than legitimise and quantify the assessment made through extended classroom contact'.

A mark or a tick will not indicate why or how the child 'succeeded' or 'failed' to gain the correct answer, the range of learning styles used or other aspects relating to the further use of this knowledge. Most of our teaching strategies and our lesson planning are built on informal assessment.

Observations and assessments can be used to assist the children when and where they need help. That is, feedback can be immediate and used in the context where the problem arose.

Problem-solving activities are central to maths within a thematic approach. Formal testing will not successfully indicate the level of competence in using appropriate materials, the ordering of the procedures to be used, the varied procedures used in different contexts, or the motivation and creativity which has been fostered.

We therefore need to structure, organise and maximise the efficiency of our observations, which may be recorded using anecdotal records or checklists. They then provide a comparison for later observations and assist the teacher when planning further activities for the children, either for consolidation or extension. They also provide the information required to report to the teachers and parents.

A wide range of checklists is possible. They may indicate a particular mathematical area covering a sequence of developmental stages, or show the personal qualities and communication skills acquired during the activities.

Assessment 1

The children were each given a different variety of 10c, 5c, 2c and 1c coins. We used photographic film canisters so that each child had his or her own mini money box.

'How much did I/you get today?'

The children loved this activity. They could pool their money with others or act independently when buying flowers for their table from the classroom flower stall. They later requested banking facilities!

As they counted and compared I could make the following observations.

	Nathan	Belinda	Nicholas	Kristy	Andrew	Holly	Leah	Ben	Dean	Straun	Chris
Sorted coins	✓	✓	✓	✓	✓	✓	✓	✓	✓	✓	X
Aware of value	✓	✓	✓	✓	✓	✓	✓	✓	X	✓	X
Counted by 5s	✓	✓	✓	✓	✓	✓	✓	✓	X	✓	X
2s	✓	✓	✓	✓	✓	✓	✓	✓	X	✓	X
1s	✓	✓	✓	✓	✓	to 30	✓	✓	✓	✓	X
Able to combine counting patterns 5 10 12 14 16 17	✓	✓	✓	✓	½	?	✓	✓	X	✓	X
Used materials to add value of coins	X	X	X	X	X	X	X	X	✓ needed to be shown		
Could exchange coins for others of equal value	✓	✓	✓	✓	✓	✓	X	✓		✓	X
Can round off to nearest 10	✓	✓	✓	✓	✓	✓	✓	✓	✓	✓	✓
Knows if sufficient amount to purchase 17c will buy 15c item	✓	✓	✓	✓	✓	✓	✓	✓	X	✓	✓
Can calculate change	✓	✓	✓	✓	✓	?	✓	✓		✓	✓

Assessment 2

The children were collecting lots of Pal dog food labels. For each label collected the company donated 10c to the 'Guide Dog Association'. This was an on-going activity and the children were involved in:
• counting the number of labels collected daily
• keeping a weekly tally
• keeping a weekly progressive tally
• recording on a graph the number of labels collected by each child
• working out how much money the labels were worth
• using the calendar to
    (a) record daily, weekly and monthly totals
    (b) block out weekends, school and public holidays, etc.
    (c) see how many days or weeks remained for collecting
    (d) see if any days were the best collection days and why.

They also investigated the following:
• Why did our string display break?
  What would be a better alternative?
• How big should our collection box be?
• Why were some labels smaller or larger?
• How many dogs did the class own?
• Why did Georgie's dog have more cans each week?
• Why did some dogs have no cans at all?

Any and all of these activities provided a wealth of assessment opportunities.

One day the children were asked how we could determine the favourite variety of dog food. The cans were clearly labelled chicken, beef, etc., as well as being colour coded. They were then asked to display this knowledge and add to it each day as more labels were collected.

Kristy   Worked with Nick to make cards indicating each 10 labels collected. Organised others to count, collect pens, etc.

Nick   Grouped labels with Kristy — checked numbers.
Indicated $1 on each label.
Lined up cards for easy reference.
Made extra cards and pegs for spare labels.

Holly   Worked alongside Leah and Andrew, then joined in.
Competent counting 1s and 10s.
Unsure 2s beyond 30.

Andrew   Put a sticker on card for each label — grouped in 10s.

Leah   Counted well. Keen to show relationship between 4 10s and 40.
Uncertain how to record 110. (100 10?). Intro. Montessori cards.

Dean   Sorted all the varieties. Then counted each pile. Not sure how to show difference although aware of greatest, smallest number. Went to calendar to see how many more labels he could bring before the holidays.

Leigh   Counted by 10s to 100. Converted to dollars. Interest in reading and adding $150 000 money signs on labels.

Assessment 3

The children were involved in a measuring activity which required them to find the length of the room using any measuring unit they liked.

Leigh   Used plastic sticks, alternating two colours then counted by 2s. Checked sticks were in a straight line.

Claire   Used long rulers. Estimated space not covered was about ½ length of ruler. Showed interest in centimetre markings. Follow up.

Olivia   Used lots of bottle tops. Found 20 tops=1 ruler of Claire's. Changed unit for easy measuring. Counted in multiples of 20.

Louise   Used stick, circle pattern.
Unconcerned about overlap.

Adam   Measured very carefully, including finger in between units! Work with Louise and Adam tomorrow.

Ben   Used string, then measured it on a metric ruler. Able to read metre and centimetre markings.

Assessment 4

The children were given a variety of objects to be party food, such as:
  10 tops (cakes)
  23 sticks (sausage rolls)
  9 cups (drink)
  12 squares (sandwiches)
Each group of four children was given a different number. They were asked to share these.

  This activity provided me with the opportunity to observe social interaction and co-operative skill abilities.

Kristy Wanted to be exact—cakes into exact halves. Cut up last 3 sausage rolls into quarters. Rather bossy.

Amy   Watched everyone working. Chattered without applying herself to the task. Only related to Leah.

Ben   Very friendly—able to share ideas well.

Karla   Very assertive. Listens well and asks others their ideas. Helped younger children by re-explaining her sharing strategies.

Collecting examples of children's work which indicate a significant stage of their development, and covering a range of mathematical approaches and areas, is a most effective way to document progress. The folio will be a cumulative record, of particular use when reporting to parents at parent–teacher interviews or in writing reports for parents or future teachers. The children can also refer to specific work of their own, to appropriate work of other children which may assist their learning, and most importantly, gauge their own performance and progress.

EXAMPLE 1

The children had been reading a magazine and one of the advertisements had given a person's weight in stones and pounds. They were rather curious about this, having only experienced weighing themselves using metric scales. One or two commented that that was how their grandmothers weighed themselves.

I was able to find bathroom scales showing both the metric and the imperial measure. The children were surprised to find that they could not convert stones to pounds using multiples of ten as in metric measure. The following are examples of their conversion methods once they had established that one stone equalled fourteen pounds.

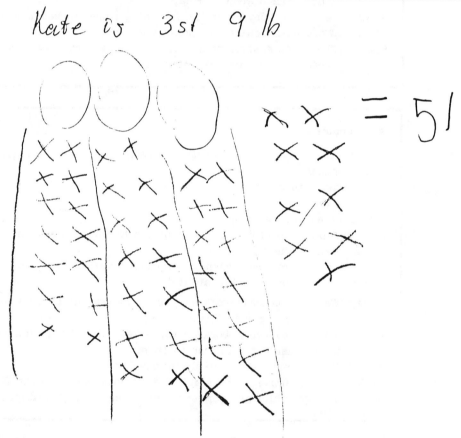

Kate is 3 st 9 lb

Kate counted by 2s throughout and found the task quite easy. She went on to find who weighed the same as herself.

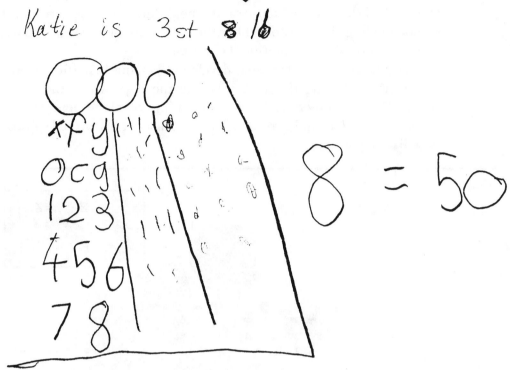

Katie thought she would write letters instead of numbers, then thought it wasn't as easy to keep count. "I had to keep counting the letters as I thought of them Then I did numbers. Sticks and dots were quicker.

Later on I showed Katie number codes. *letter and* She then taught everyone else!

EXAMPLE 2

In the story on the next page Marianne has shown her ability to use large numbers, e.g. 30. Initially she used the process of subtraction, then realised that she could incorporate multiplication. She was then able to take the answer (6) and continue her story using both subtraction and division. She decided on the bracket for 6-2 as she said they needed to 'be done first'. When she finished this particular area of her work we explored all the 'bracket' fixtures that held things together around the school building. I then showed her the formal use of brackets. We were joined by several other interested children.

The following day Marianne developed her mathematical recordings further, sharing the apples among the pigs, where they would be on the tree branches, the number of legs on three pigs (3x4=), the number of eyes and ears (3x2=), etc. She later discovered spirals — 'just like a pig's tail'.

$$30 - 20 - 2 - 2 = 6$$
$$30 - 20 - 2 \times 2 = 6$$
$$6 - 2 \div 2 = 2$$

As mother pig and her two babies
came walking along they found an apple tree.
There were thirty apples on it. The mother ate
twenty but the two little pigs only ate two each.
They weren't feeling very hungry.
Maybe tomorrow they will eat the rest.

If they leave two for their mum,
how many will they get?

Marianne.

EXAMPLE 3

I went into my garden one cool, sunny
morning to find that Spring had arrived.
Some flowers were out.

Can you make my garden?

I saw 3 flowers with 4 petals each.
Then I found another 2 flowers. They had
6 petals each.

    WH!!   WH!!
            The wind blew 2 petals away!

Then I found another 2 flowers. These
had 5 petals on them.

I set this task to determine the children's understanding of grouping. I did not ask them to count the petals; that came from their
own interest.

- Holly was most definite in her setting out of the flowers, often checking the number of petals and making sure they were centred together.
  After pasting, she removed the two petals blown by the wind. She
  preferred to calculate the number of petals mentally.
- Kate drew the centres of the flowers first, then went back to add
  the appropriate number of petals. She saved the last two leaves she
  was pasting to be those the wind had blown. Then she numbered
  her petals, as she discovered she was counting petals 'forever'. I noted
  Kate's need for assistance with recording number symbols. Although
  verbally confident, she sought my help to record
  $34 - 2 = 32$.
- Andrew was systematic. He recorded his flower groupings as he went.

$3 \times 4 = 12$
$2 \times 6 = 12$

He immediately placed the two petals blown by the wind at the
bottom of the stem.

$2 \times 5 = 10$

He then realised that two groupings had the total of twelve petals each and went on to further recordings. He spent intervals throughout the next two days telling me how he had written this. His fascination was with the answer twelve. He has now discovered other multiples for twelve as well as being the instigator for a group of children to develop the twelve times table. This has shown me his understanding of the inter-relationship of numbers and processes.

EXAMPLE 4

We were recording the number of Pal dog food labels the children collected each day.

On this particular day I asked the children to work out their answer and then to explain the procedures they used.

We all benefited from sharing the many different ways of adding the equation shown opposite. Very few children had actually added in sequence. Their methods showed me their abilities in adding, grouping numbers in 10s, in rounding numbers to the nearest 10 and their understanding of place value.

Involving children in assessment

Recording assessment results and collecting representative examples of work should be the task of both the teacher and the student.

In the stimulating classroom environment — implicit in the thematic approach — the children will be eager to share their assessments with each other. In place of 'I got the right answer but Peter didn't', is the attitude of sharing results, of explaining the processes used to gain those results to the child who wasn't as successful in performing or understanding the problem. A sense of failure is not a feature here;

How do you work out

$$2 + 2 + 17 + 3 + 5$$

?

Monday 4 Sep.

- $17 + \underset{4}{2+2} + \underset{8}{3+5}$

- $17 + 4 + 8 = 29$

- $\underset{8}{3+5} + \underset{4}{2+2} = 12 + 17$

- $\underset{7}{2+5} + \underset{5}{3+2}$ (17) $5+5+6+1$

- $10 + \underset{}{2+2} + \underset{8}{3+5} + 7 = 29$

- $\underset{20}{17+3} + \underset{9}{2+2+5} = 29$

- $\underset{10}{2+3+5} + \underset{27}{17} + 2 = 29$

rather there is a sense of motivation to pursue this line of thought again and in similar situations until success is achieved.

By sharing in this type of assessment the children learn to approach new problems with the knowledge that they may, or may not, succeed initially. They may need to seek guidance and assistance from others, and find new materials or ideas to help them, but they will approach new activities with confidence and enjoy their mathematics. As they discover or accomplish a new concept or skill, they often initiate the teaching of this to other children.

As they work, I encourage the children to ask questions of themselves, myself and other children. These questions help me to understand their thought processes and to provide the link between our two realms of understanding.

Children's questions should be well thought out. I discuss their questions with the children themselves and with other children.

'Has this question helped us solve the question at hand?'

'Does it lead to another area of study?'

'Should we write it down and come back to it?'

'Can we divert for a moment, then return to the first question?'

Older children will naturally handle the discussion on the art of questioning in greater depth, but it is important to lead children to be discerning with their questions from as early an age as possible. Toddlers constantly ask 'Why?' It is natural to extend this line of questioning.

Leading children to ask meaningful questions helps not only the teacher in assessing the students — and the teaching techniques — but assists the children to develop their own problem-solving strategies, thought processes and self-assessment procedures.

Listening skills

Using a thematic approach provides the basis for a wonderful exchange of ideas and methods. To gain the most benefit we must all listen. While the children have always been expected to listen to the teacher, the reverse has not always been implicit in our daily teaching. What we should strive toward is a sharing of ideas and of listening time from child to teacher, teacher to child and child to child.

The development of our listening skills will usually go hand in hand with the development of our questioning skills.

As we listen to each other, we need to develop the 'quality' of listening.

'Why is she saying this?'

'What else is he thinking, or has thought, to make such a statement?'

EXAMPLE

During an activity on measuring, the children were recording their own heights. They had easily determined the tallest and shortest in the grade and were anxious to find the second tallest, about which there was some dissenting discussion. Two boys measured 1.31 metres.

Danny: They are both the same so they go together.

Katie: But Alexander doesn't look the same.

Danny: Look. I'll show you. They are the same.(Alexander and Karl were remeasured, with the same result.)

Katie: I know it says that, but I think Karl should be second.

Danny (quite frustrated by now): But they are the same so it doesn't matter.

Katie: I know, but Karl is bigger and so is his dad. (Katie spread her arms horizontally to enforce her idea.)

Whereas Danny had focused specifically on measuring and recording the children's height, Katie had projected the problem further. This was initially unspoken and quite possibly not fully formed in her own mind, but by saying that Karl was 'bigger' she was comparing not only height but weight. Hence her reasoning for Karl to be second. She had also projected to his possible future height as his father was in fact much taller than Alexander's father.

From this discussion I was able to help the children explain their ideas to each other. We debated this at the class level, deciding to give the two boys equal height status. One group of children then went on to compare both height and weight—they ended up using a points system for centimetres and kilograms. Another group pursued the concept of 'How tall am I in relation to my mother and father?' and a third group 'Do children usually grow taller than their parents?' This last activity became a far-reaching family activity involving aunts, cousins and grandparents.

Body language

Body language is implicit in questioning and listening. Katie's explanation of Karl being bigger was accompanied by her hands stretching out to the side. It showed she meant 'bigger' not 'taller' specifically. Danny's nod of the head meant 'yes'—now he realised what she had been trying to explain.

Children's facial expressions and hand movements can often express so much to the observant teacher. They are another means of communication. The confident to the puzzled to the harassed look. The eagerness to move someone else's construction piece to where it will be successfully balanced or joined. The shuffling of or hesitation to move concrete equipment, or to record without first checking with someone else's work indicates a child's level of competence and the perception of his or her own ability at the task.

Teachers need to respond, not only with questioning and listening, but also by using their own body language to its greatest advantage.

'It doesn't matter. Have another try.'

A shrug and a despairing look as you move to the next child, or a grin, a shrug and you move to observe their activity convey messages to the children. Which would you, as the learner, respond most positively to? Each child will respond in an individual way. You will know which response will be most effective with each child.

Photos and videos

Photographs can be taken of construction activities. They are useful to show large or group recording activities which are too cumbersome or unable to be filed effectively.

A videotape is another medium for assessment and is often extremely useful for children to assess themselves. I have also found that they are keen to take the videos home to show their families. They are definitely amateur productions, but everyone benefits from the interchange of ideas. Interested but often very busy parents welcome the opportunity to experience with their children the day-to-day activities at school. Videos can also be used to gauge the children's progress over several months.

In summary then, the more informal anecdotal methods of assessment — observation, continuous records of work, dialogues with children, their own questions, photographs and videos — can provide a wealth of information about a child's personal mathematical development. Notes, work examples, checklists and videos in particular can be used to discuss progress with other teachers and parents.

◆

4

ORGANISING
THE CLASSROOM

◆

Providing maths equipment

To provide children with a wide range of mathematical experiences, to encourage self-motivation and divergent, creative learning patterns, there is a real need to provide lots of concrete materials, both formal and informal, for the children and teacher to use.

However, it is not necessary to purchase expensive mathematical equipment before beginning your maths theme — and it is even preferable not to. When planning a thematic approach consideration should be given to:

- the maths equipment already in the school
- other equipment in the school useful for the maths programme
- household 'junk' items
- financial resources available
- access to offcuts, factory reject materials
- storage areas
- access to equipment
- classroom furniture arrangements

There is usually a wealth of equipment throughout a school, although sometimes not always conspicuous or accessible. If you have not already done so, you need to seek out *all* equipment and compile an inventory. The bits and pieces you may be tempted to leave in a cupboard or to discard may be just the pieces needed to complete a set of equipment in someone else's cupboard.

Evaluation of school mathematical resources should not be restricted to those listed under mathematical equipment in the catalogues.

Many art supplies are ideal when exploring your maths theme, e.g. pop sticks, polystyrene shapes, play dough, various materials for patterning, etc. Paper, paint and other assorted materials are essential when recording and representing mathematical findings. The supermarket, stationers and hardware suppliers have many appropriate items: pictures, paper cups, resealable plastic bags, nails, wood offcuts, etc.

Manipulative equipment such as Struts, Constructo Straws, Timberlock, Lego, Nuts and Bolts, etc. is invaluable. Construction activities can be made challenging, for example, by asking children to build a bridge strong enough for a truck carrying six building blocks. To accomplish such tasks knowledge or investigation of many aspects of space and measurement will be essential.

Many items discarded in the home, such as bottle tops, lids, cartons, provide a ready resource of mathematical equipment. They are easily replaced if lost or broken and are familiar to the children. They can be pasted onto paper or into models to make permanent displays or records of achievement. At home the children can show their parents what they have accomplished during the day, without needing to seek a replacement item for specialised school equipment.

Advertise regularly throughout the year, in the school newsletter for the items you need and have your containers ready.

EXAMPLE

Dear Parents,

Thank you to all the families who sent along the 'junk' we were seeking for maths and art supplies. We have had lots of fun using it already. For this week:

YES PLEASE	NO MORE THANKS
cardboard offcuts	margarine containers
lemonade lids	small boxes
pop tops	egg cartons
texta tops	straws
paper cups	
bread tags	
spraycan lids	

Many factory owners are delighted to provide schools with suitable offcuts of material, e.g. polystyrene packaging, vinyl scraps (to cut into tangram shapes, attribute shapes, etc.), plastic moulds, etc. Many parents also have access to materials at their place of employment. However, if the material is inappropriate, thank the contributor then refuse politely or discard it discreetly. Be selective — don't just collect junk!

As you collect resource materials encourage the children to use and experiment with them. Be imaginative and creative. A bottle top can be a fairy's cup, a balloon or home base of the softball court.

The following list will provide a starting point for a maths equipment collection.

Basic equipment
coloured paper squares in assorted sizes
pencils, pens, Textas
magazines
newspapers
containers — margarine, yoghurt, ice-cream, wine (casks)
scissors
tape, pins, pegs

Commercial materials
plastic squares
plastic sticks
counters
Unifix materials
M.A.B. base-ten blocks
plasticene or play dough
beads
animal shapes — farm, sealife, dinosaurs, etc.
transport shapes
(I find it preferable to have larger quantities of a few shapes than a very wide range with not enough of each for comparisons to be made)
interlocking blocks — Lego, Timberlock, Struts
scales — large, well-balanced
measuring tapes
capacity and volume measures
construction and manipulative equipment — enough to be used!
money packs
jigsaws, puzzles, games

Informal materials
polystyrene cups
soft drink lids
milk lids and circle seals
cotton reels
Pears shampoo bottles (for use as building blocks)
flip-top lids — toothpaste, detergent, shampoo
bread tags
junk mail catalogues
straws
patty papers

pop sticks
slide photo frames
spraycan lids
clocks
sand tray — assorted bottle, jugs, spoons, lids
beans
string, wool, tape
paper bags
any assortment of shapes in card, plastic, wood
take-away pizza lids, paper plates
Texta lids
Biro lids

Teacher's display materials

a selection of precut coloured card or cover paper
  A4 and A3 sizes
  flashcard strips, two or three different sizes
scrap paper
felt-tip marking pens — assorted colours and sizes
paste, glue, spray adhesive
scissors
display materials — pegs, Blu-Tack, pins, paper clips
coat hangers, circular indoor clothes hanger
large card
contact adhesive
pictures, magazines, story books
blank dice, markers, playing cards

Lots of other materials can be collected at different times, e.g. stamps, coins, etc. Some items may only be applicable or of value during one particular theme. Remember to discard inappropriate or excess items.

Planning and identifying priorities

If your school needs more resources but has limited funding, you should consider whether one area of maths equipment can be given higher priority than another. Forward planning should cover more than just the first twelve months. For example, one balance pan for weighing may be a wasted purchase. It may be more feasible to purchase ten in the first year then concentrate spending in a different area the following year.

Perhaps the best way to start is by considering the items you need to:
- make your equipment resources adequate
- provide technical or more accurate measurement activities
- complement existing equipment.

Place these in priority order for presentation to your school finance committee. You may consider other fund-raising committees, activities or private business sources you could approach.

Be aware of the availability of consultants within the education system and from private enterprise. They will willingly provide in-service activities using the school's current equipment or with new materials available for consideration of purchase.

Storage

At this stage you may need to discuss with all school staff the storage and use of the equipment.

- Will it be stored in a central area and a borrowing system operate?
- Will borrowing be long term, short term or both?
- Will some equipment remain in the classroom throughout the term or the year?
- Who will supervise the maths store and the borrowing system?
- Who will be in charge of forward planning for further purchases, repairs, replacements, etc.?
- Should some equipment be combined or separated to make it more useful or accessible? For example, should Unifix blocks be stored in ice-cream containers, with several containers per room, or in one large crate? One set of balance scales may be better shared centrally. When required, all children in the class could have immediate 'hands on' experience. You may have sufficient equipment to provide for both systems.

When you have your equipment together, be selective in the choice of containers for the storage of both large and small items. This can be paramount to the success of your borrowing scheme. Questions to assist your planning are:

- Can items be easily carried?
- Do containers need lids, labels or colour coding?
- Are they durable?
- Can they be replaced if necessary?
- Do they fit on existing shelving?

The stackable plastic cubes available at most supermarkets and large department stores have proved to be very useful. If finances are restricted, alternatives such as ice-cream and margarine containers, polystyrene fruit cases and orange mesh bags (with a draw string threaded through the top) are an excellent substitute.

Within the classroom the equipment should be easily accessible to the children.

Hand the responsibility of caring for the materials to the children. Discuss where they would best be stored, then expect the children to be responsible for collecting and returning the equipment they use. In group situations they should share the responsibility. Children who have only a few items to pack away should be encouraged to assist someone with lots. They may be grateful for assistance the following day!

To rely on the system of monitors putting out and returning equipment could stifle the children's initiative and creativity. As they go to collect their equipment they may find something more appropriate or challenging or that they haven't seen before. Initially it may be necessary to remind some children of their responsibility to the class and to you in sharing and packing away.

Using equipment

I encourage the children to use our materials at any time to assist in creating or developing concrete interpretations of their own or given situations.

When presenting new situations I select a number of appropriate materials and encourage the children to use them according to their needs. If any of the materials become inappropriate (cumbersome, too small, not enough, inexact, etc.) we discuss the problem and feel free to discard these and begin our activity again, using a more suitable material.

It is necessary to establish the need for selecting suitable equipment before beginning an activity. If the children do not select carefully, then keep changing, little will be accomplished. However, I have found that most children are keen to get results and very quickly discriminate in their choice of materials.

I try to use as wide a variety of materials as possible on a daily basis to provide a role model for the children. They know I enjoy finding new uses for equipment and are delighted to show me a new way to represent their work.

Using 'junk' materials

EXAMPLE: BREAD TAGS

1 Use as a supplement to commercial counting materials.

96   97   98

2 Sort them according to colours or size.
3 Make a colour pattern.

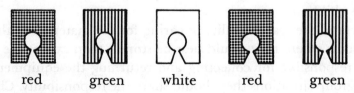

red   green   white   red   green

4 Link them up.
Who has the longest chain?

46

If they are the same length, do they have the same number of tags?

5 Sort them into days, months or years.
   Sequence them according to the printed date.
   In which month did we collect the most?
   Which day did we collect the most?

6 Estimation — how many tags in a handful, and a cupful?

7 Weight — how many equal one bottle lid?

8 Area — how many tags cover your hand, chair, etc.?

9 Use them to replace commercial counters or squares when record-ing work. They glue easily and are a fun alternative to paper. They are also easily replaced.

10 Make a shape direction pattern.

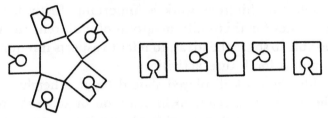

11 Length — how many to one metre?
   How far can we flip them?

12 Place value — hang them in tens along a stick.

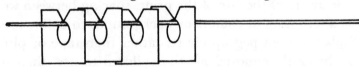

How many sticks of 10 can I make from 34 tags?

13 Grouping or multiplication and division — stack 5 tags on each of 7 cotton reels.

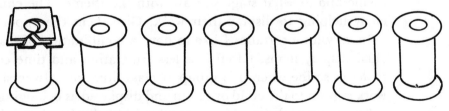

14 Put 4 tags on each of the branches of a tree? What would you call this tree?

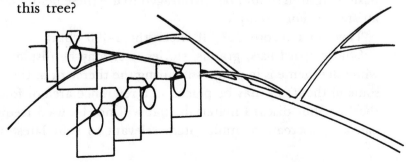

15 These tags are miniature sandwiches. Can you share them with your friends? (Each child could be given a small handful, to extend the possibilities.)

Organising the furniture

Consideration should be given to the arrangement of larger furniture in the classroom — tables, lockers, trolleys, etc. Can they act as dividers or storage areas? Should, or could, they be rearranged to provide a different setting for a new theme?

Wall space and display surfaces

Display of children's work is important, firstly for the confidence it generates for that child or group of children, then for the others to be able to share the ideas, to refer to aspects if required and to provide stimulus for future activities.

Ideally, work displayed should be at a height where it is easy for the children to read, to indicate on or to work from. This is often not possible to achieve without becoming encompassed by a cardboard jungle. As an alternative I try to ensure displays are made attractive and legible.

Be aware of the size of the print, spacing between words and lines, the alternating of colours or backgrounds to define areas of work on display. I often peg up charts rather than tape or pin them as they can be easily removed for the children to use, then replaced.

Keep the display changing. I attempt to change at least one item each day, such as adding another question to a problem-solving activity. The amount and type of display material will depend on your theme and at what stage you are with the theme. The children will enjoy helping to display their work. Give them the opportunity.

In very junior grades I like to have a combination of teacher and child display items. Often it is less frustrating and time consuming to act as scribe when in a group or class situation. Ownership of this work is given to the child or group and displayed as belonging to them.

Some materials (teaching aids) should be displayed on a long-term basis. Children should be encouraged to use these before seeking other assistance. For example:

'How do I record 39? I'll check the 1-100 chart.'

Charts, word lists, graphs, stories, etc. may be displayed centrally while the theme is in progress. During the theme or at the conclusion, some of the items may be placed in a reference area or folder for further use, but discard materials that will not be used frequently. You can always create a similar item relevant to your latest studies.

Allow your maths display to be part of your language display, or ideally of your total, integrated display.

While you participate in maths activities with the children, have your card, textas, markers, paste, etc. easily accessible and ready for use by you or the children as you discuss, build, consider, etc.

PART TWO:

THEMES
AND ACTIVITIES

INTRODUCTION

The themes outlined in this book have been chosen to illustrate the variety of mathematical areas that may be developed. Each theme was introduced in a manner appropriate to its own atmosphere and style. Situations from which these can develop are:

- an art activity
- a special event
- a news or other media item
- a general studies, music or science activity
- an excursion
- a special school function, e.g. school fete
- building models using manipulative equipment
- an informal discussion with the children
- a fantasy or make-believe situation.

This range of possibilities is ever-widening and may develop through:

- children's interest, either individual or group
- teacher instigation—having previously gauged a common interest or need.

The amount of time spent on the theme will always vary. It will depend on:

- the children's interest
- any previous involvement with the same theme
- the possible change of direction to a more fruitful theme
- the need for the children to cover the specific area of mathematics being explored

● the range of mathematical opportunity afforded.

In this section of the book I have detailed many, but by no means all, the activities the children and I have engaged in throughout the various themes. Knowing your own class of children and their individual abilities, you are the best person to determine which avenue is most likely to benefit them. You can then develop other minor facets for groups or individuals.

I have used many of these activities at all levels of the primary school. Children of all ages love, and benefit greatly from, using a range of concrete materials. They need these whenever they are exploring any new concept or skill. Any of the activities can be adapted to suit children of any age. The older the children, the more detail and variation you are able to offer. If you listen to the children and observe their responses you will be able to provide lots of experiences at their particular level.

When planning, and throughout the development of the theme, I keep a checklist of the areas I have covered, or that may be possible (see Appendix). This ensures that I maintain an even balance of all mathematical areas. If any have not been covered at all or not in sufficient detail, I then plan themes which will readily lend themselves to overcoming this shortfall.

Plan your introduction and enjoy your mathematics!

◆

DRAGONS

◆

No matter what the age or year level, I have found when dragons are mentioned all children's — and most adults' — eyes start to twinkle. For many years I have seen such interesting language work arise from this theme, and I found it was easy to incorporate mathematics as well.

Building a dragon

James had been telling us about his outing to the Chinese New Year celebrations. He was most impressed by the noise and the size of the dragon. Richard and Jessie both knew the song 'Puff, the Magic Dragon'. Our interest high, we planned to make our dragon. Would it be a class, a group or an individual activity? Should the dragon be long, huge, friendly or cross? It was decided that a dragon had to be huge, so it would need all our combined efforts.

The next day, surrounded with numerous supermarket boxes we had collected, we began constructing our dragon — sorting, grouping, comparing and counting as we shared our ideas. We stacked and balanced the boxes in various ways before coming to our final 'dragon' structure. We had decided on:
- the size of his legs, comparing front and back
- where the head should be positioned
- which boxes best suited the shape we wanted
- how to make boxes into feet
- where to cut boxes to alter their shape or size without losing strength
- how best to join boxes to gain maximum balance and strength.
Now what should he look like?

There was a wealth of creative ideas. If only we could have used them all! (A few weeks later the children made smaller box construction models individually and in pairs, using many of these original ideas.)

The children were keen to continue the same day, but I felt we needed to share our ideas and arrive at decisions as to how they could be carried out. We needed thinking time, and time to collect the resources we would need. The benefit of this was proved. The following day our ideas came together very easily. Our dragon had:

- chequerboard feet
- alternating circle pattern sides, like scales
- striped legs
- large scales on his back graduating down in size to the tip of his tail
- a patterned pink and silver 'patty pan' chest (We estimated how many we would need of all of the above and had fun seeing who was the closest. Lots of revisions were made during the process and our estimation skills vastly improved.)
- furry ears
- two large and two small eyes
- fiery nostrils
- both sides of his body looking the same.

Other finishing touches were added in the days that followed.

During this time the children had needed to:

- cover the boxes with coloured paper squares
- ensure the scales along the body were the same size and shape within the specified areas
- overlap the scales and make them stand out
- keep the patterns uniform (This was made more difficult when the chequerboard pattern on the feet went around corners, and when it joined. How and where could the join be best disguised, as the last squares were too long?)
- keep the scales along the back standing up
- work out how to join the eyes to the boxes—being heavy plastic lids they wouldn't glue!

One of the major benefits of all this activity was that the children learnt to stand back, think, observe, consider, then tackle the next problem. They needed to proceed systematically while still keeping an open mind for other, or unexpected, eventualities. That's mathematics!

During the following week, the dragon was used as a focus for most of our language work—story telling, literature, creative writing, reading and drama. Each day we also focused on a mathematical aspect of the dragon. For several days the children were interested in counting and comparing his scales.

tail + back + 4 × legs =
round + square + rectangle + patty pans =
green + blue + pink + silver + black + white

They classified, sorted and demonstrated to me and to their peers their numerous counting strategies and abilities.

Where to next?

The children were writing their own dragon adventure books. Following a discussion with some of them, deciding which sort of dragon they would like to be, we looked at types of scales. The children were also thinking of making dragons, as they suggested they could use pasta shapes or lollies for scales. These dragons would come to an untimely end, which involved lots of subtraction!

Another child suggested that coins would make great scales. I knew the children needed more experience in the area of money so I deliberately encouraged this suggestion.

Using some coins I had, we made the shape of a dragon. The silver coins were his back scales, the small one cent coins his claws and the two cent pieces his body. We photocopied this, then changed his appearance, still using the same coins.

Keen to continue, the children suggested bringing coins to school for the following day's activities. To avoid too many money boxes at school we decided we would all bring ten cents. This also gave me a teaching focus besides counting strategies. How many ways can ten cents be represented?

'What if Mum doesn't have a ten cent?' said Kristy.

'Then bring two five cents', said Geoffrey.

We thought we would see how many different ways they could bring ten cents. The children were following through their own suggestion!

We had many different combinations of coins the following morning. We recorded these using a rubber coin stamp. The children also graphed the number of coins collected.

Suddenly they realised the importance of value relationships. The two cent column had the most coins but not the highest value. Two five cents were the same as five two cents or

$$2 \times 5 = 5 + 5$$

Some children pursued this concept

$$1 \times 10 = 10 \times 1$$
$$2 \times 10 = 10 \times 2$$

and further to

$$5 + 5 = 2 \times 2 + 1 + 5$$

We created fifty cent dragons and ninety cent dragons! Would a ninety cent dragon have to be bigger than a fifty cent dragon?

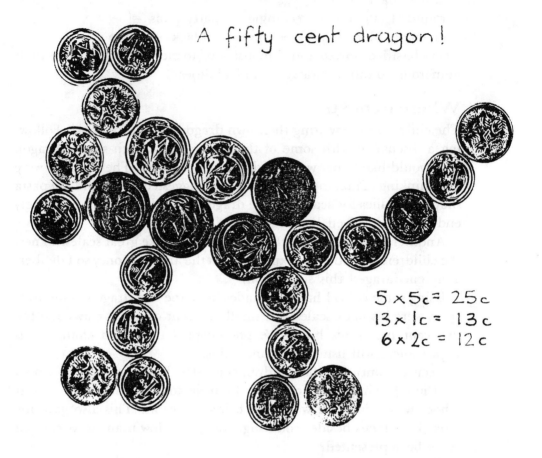

A fifty cent dragon!

$$5 \times 5c = 25c$$
$$13 \times 1c = 13c$$
$$6 \times 2c = 12c$$

We printed the dragons we made and were able to compare them at a later date, as well as while we were making them. (I was able to make an unplanned assessment of the children's spatial relations skills when they were using the stamps to print their dragons. How close to the original was the printed copy?)

Our own dragon game
Would you like to go to a dragon's birthday party?

I had some birthday wrapping paper with dragons on it. We cut these out and created our own story around the different pictures. This became a dice board game. The children played and created:
- a pathway
- alternative routes
- surprise stops—both pleasant and unpleasant (They found they needed a balance of these to prevent the game becoming negative. They also needed to be well spaced and not too exaggerated.)
- a set of clear, concise instructions
- an attractive layout.

Various strategies the children had learned in making this game and in playing commerical games at home and at school were later demonstrated as they planned and made other board games to complement our theme work.

I could have continued the dragon theme in other areas but felt that it was time to move to another theme before the children became bored. However I did allow them to refer back to areas of this work or explore further, in their own time, some of the other suggestions that had been made during our 'dragon time'. Dragons did occasionally join us in the middle of later theme work!

At the same time, and in the weeks following the dragon theme in my class, I was working with teachers in a number of other schools at varying grade levels. They were interested in starting a thematic approach to maths and I was asked to help with 'dragon maths' in their classes. They liked dragons too, and it was a fun theme to interest their children.

The teacher of a group of seven and eight year olds was interested to see her children involved in problem-solving situations and felt that she wanted maths to provide interest and a challenge, rather than being just computative exercises. We introduced the dragon theme.

What would a dragon eat?

Arriving in the class with two empty litre milk cartons, I immediately aroused the children's interest. What was I doing with them? Were we going to make something? Didn't I know where the rubbish bin was?

I explained how they were my friend Gobble-O the dragon's milk ration for the day, and went on to describe what he had eaten for the week:

10 loaves bread (21 slices in each)
7 kilograms potatoes (5 per kilogram)
4 tins drinking chocolate (how many spoonfuls?)
7 lettuce
53 tomatoes
14 litres milk

The children spontaneously started to work out what would be on his plate. The multiples of seven — one for each day of the week — were easy and provided the initial confidence and feeling of success. Then they had the harder application of determining for themselves how to share the bread, tomatoes and drinking chocolate. First they used estimation, then concrete materials. Polystyrene squares for bread, lids for tomatoes and tins of sand for drinking chocolate.

The following day we asked them to write out Gobble-O's shopping list, as he had changed his weekly menu. Each day he ate:
Breakfast 2 Weet-Bix, 4 slices toast

Lunch	1 can baked beans, 2 slices toast

Lunch   1 can baked beans, 2 slices toast
an apple and an orange
Dinner   2 chops, 3 potatoes, 10 beans, 4 carrots,
2 scoops ice-cream, 2 bananas and ½ bottle topping
Supper   3 slices cake and ½ fruit bun

The children needed to multiply all these by seven, then in order to write my shopping list they had to find out:

- How many Weet-Bix to a box and state which sized box I should buy.
- How many slices of bread to a loaf, and again which sized loaf.

$$4 + 4 + 4 + 4 + 4 + 4 + 4 = 28$$
$$8 + 8 + 8 + 4 = 28$$
$$16 + 12 = 28$$
$$20 + 8 = 28$$

Megan's work shows the strategies she used as she calculated how many slices of bread would be needed for breakfast for the week. She initially counted

$$4 + 4 + 4 + 4 + 4 + 4 + 4 = 28$$

and seemed rather uncertain. When I asked was she sure, she replied, 'I think so'. She then went on with the further recordings. At the end she was completely satisfied and self-assured. She *knew* seven fours were twenty-eight. Other children in her group had determined which food product they were going to calculate. Then the list was to be a combined effort.

As they wrote their shopping list, Darren and Lisa multiplied by seven. They confidently ticked their answers when they checked with other children. When they came to the halves they knew how to write

$7 \times \frac{1}{2}$

'Because that's a half (pointing to the symbol) and it's seven times.'

'But when I add it I get ten halves and it doesn't sound right', said Lisa. 'How do I work it out?'

$7 \times \frac{1}{2}$ Lisa had added the digits

$7 + 1 + 2 = 10/2$

1" B. 2 weet bix 7×2=14 ✓
. 4 slices bread 7×4=28 ✓

Darren and
Lisa

L. 1 can baked beans 7×1=7 ✓
2. slices toast 7×2=14 ✓
1 apple 1 orange 7×2=14 ✓

T. 2 chops 7×2=14 ✓
3 potatoes 7×3=21 ✓
10 beans 7×10=70. ✓
4 carrots 7×4=28 ✓
2 scoops ice cream 7×2=14 ✓
2 bananas 7×2=14 ✓
½ bottle choc. syrup 7×1   4 bottles
S. 3 slices cake 7×3=21   3½
½ boston bun 7×½ =   3½

Working together, we used concrete materials initially, then Lisa and Darren were keen to draw the halves on the shopping list. (Their teacher noted that this would be a good mathematical learning experience to incorporate into the coming week's activities. Both children were obviously ready to explore fractions.)

2 weet bixs 7×2=14
4 slices bread 7×4=28
can baked beans 7×1=7
2 slices toast 7×2=14
apple 7×1=7 orange 7×1=
2 chops 7×2=14
3 potatoes 7×3=21

10 beans 7×10=70
4 carrots 7×4=28
2 scoops ice cream 7×2=14
½ bottle choc syrup = 4
3 slices cake 7×3=21
½ bosto bun = 4

claire and Nicole

Claire and Nicole showed that they understood $7 \times \frac{1}{2}$ as well as realising they could not purchase half a bottle of topping or half a fruit bun. They also combined the two amounts of bread.

When I asked about buying fourteen scoops of ice-cream they were immediately ready to suggest that we could estimate the number of scoops of ice-cream in the container and count the slices of bread and number of Weet-Bix at the supermarket. Otherwise I would need to wait another day until they went home and found out.

These two girls were obviously ready for more difficult mathematical challenges, so we provided them with some supermarket advertising pamphlets and asked them to plan and cost the following week's shopping. They later went on to plan a Dragon Party for Gobble-O. What fun to plan, cost and *have* a Dragon Party!

While they did need assistance from time to time, the teacher had more time to work with the children needing more detailed guidance at this time.

How big are dragons?

In a class of five and six year olds we collected lots of different dragons. We found similarities, differences, ordered them according to size, grouped them, etc.

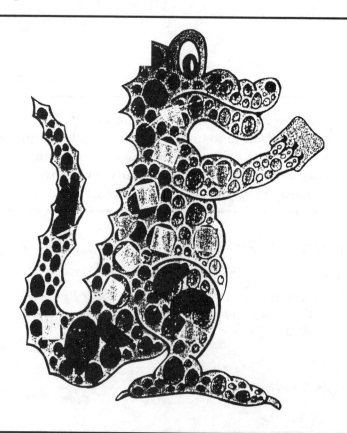

4 big + 3 little = 7 dragons
6 big and 2 little, take away the 4 that went into the cave, so 4 are left
6 + 2 − 4 = 4

A painted dragon

A group of six and seven year old children enjoyed working out how much their dragons had to pay to be painted with different coloured spots.

purple = 2 cents
blue = 5 cents
green = 10 cents

Then we changed the cost of the colours. Would they still be worth the same? When Christopher said his dragon still paid the same, he was strongly challenged. After much recounting they finally agreed with him. But why? Later on, after trying more cards and repeating many they had already used, they realised Christopher's was the only dragon with the same number of spots for each colour. If they had not reached this conclusion I had thought of asking them to write out the painter's invoices. During the recording of these they may have visually seen the difference.

I later used the same activity with ten and eleven year old children to provide an experience for fast, mental computation.

We then changed the amounts charged for the painted spots to $1.89, $3.87 and $2.78. We wanted practice in multiplying by 7, 8 and 9.

As well, we were using decimal points and place value with larger numbers.

Where can a dragon fit?

Another class of six and seven year old children explored area, using the dragon theme. They made large footprints then explored:

- How many dragons could stand in this paddock
    — standing on two feet
    — standing on four feet?
- What if they want to lie down?
- Can the dragon stand in this paddock without squashing the flowers? (We initially did this using large plastic shapes for flowers and our cut-out feet. Later I provided a range of cards with flowers and the children could stamp feet on these, using them under acetate sheets.)
- How large are your feet in comparison to your height? So how tall would our dragon be?
- Using the feet cut-outs, how many orange dragons or red dragons could stand in your classroom?

The teachers and I found it was usually quite easy to listen to the children's discussions and to channel their interests to an area from which we felt they would benefit, given further experiences. At the same time we covered nearly all mathematical areas in conjunction with the chosen area.

Our Environment

Nature is mathematics

We are immersed in our environment. We should lead the children to explore and become fully aware of all that is constantly happening around us. There are so many mathematics principles involved in nature.

Example

The 'Fibonacci numbers'

  1 1 2 3 5 8 13 21 34 55 89 144...

are very interesting and we find them in many places in art and nature. If we divide any number by the number on its right we get

$$\frac{1}{1} \quad \frac{1}{2} \quad \frac{2}{3} \quad \frac{3}{5} \quad \frac{5}{8} \quad \frac{8}{13} \quad \frac{13}{21} \quad \frac{21}{34} \quad \frac{34}{55}$$

'These fractions are related to the growth of plants. When new leaves grow from the stem of a plant, they spiral around the stem. The spiral turns as it climbs. The amount of turning from one leaf to the next is a fraction of a complete rotation around the stem. This fraction is always one of the Fibonacci fractions.' (Irving Adler)

  Pine cones have Fibonacci ratios of 5/8, 8/13. Daisies usually have the Fibonacci ratio of 21/34.

Not only is the study of our environment of benefit to us mathematically, as in many other areas, but it is both constant and ever-changing and most of all enjoyable.

What's in the pond?

Most of us recall the delightful times we have had — and still enjoy — paddling in a pond, creek or river. This relatively small part of our environment provides a wealth of interesting areas for study — fauna and flora studies, aquatic life, soil movement or erosion and flooding, to name just a few.

Caitlin and Curtis had brought some tadpoles to school and the children were concerned that they be kept in an appropriate environment, rather than the glass jars they arrived in. This led to our study of pond life and all the environmental factors influencing either its development or destruction. The number of inhabitants in relation to its size was a major issue under discussion. Concern about contamination of the environment was spearheaded by reading *The Pond That Turned Into A Puddle*, by Jeanette Morris.

This book tells of all the rubbish that is dumped into the pond over a period of time and how this affects the inhabitants. There is not enough space, oil kills some of the weeds, the water is polluted, affecting the fish, and the children visiting the pond can no longer safely play along the edges.

I used this book as the springboard for a combined science–maths study. We made our own pond — a large plastic storage tub — and saw how much fresh water it held, marking the level to which we had filled it. During the next few weeks we added our own rubbish to the pond: an empty soft drink can, a sauce bottle, bread, chop bones and fat. This simulated a country barbecue. Then a toy car, chips and popcorn, and a load of clay were added.

The children studied and measured the effect of adding these objects to the water:

- the changing water levels

- the effect of the objects — was it immediate, long-term or both?

    We observed that the can became rusty, sauce from the bottle spread rapidly and the clay took up space, buried plants, then spread over a wider area.

Each week we took a sample of the water for comparison studies. We also considered rainfall, water run-off and evaporation. When we took our tub outside we found the birds drank from it — as well as a loitering dog! We needed to consider how much water animals living near the pond would drink.

A small group of children undertook to measure how much water each of their pets and our class pets drank. Was it always the same amount? What factors influenced the differences?

Frog fun!

We made our room into a pond and its immediate environment — river bank, shrubs, trees and rocks. Having tadpoles, we focused on frogs. To have attempted to study all the pond life in detail would have been very involved and therefore quite confusing to the children. While aware of the multiplicity of other factors, I wished the children to be able to pursue one direct line of thought and to understand and evaluate the results.

With the pond boundary firmly established for that particular day by writing tables (the river bank where it's deep) and tape (where you can wade in), we wanted to see if we (the frogs) could fit in our pond.

First, the children found they all covered approximately half the area. So they moved from the back and came to fill up the pond. They all took two spaces and two children had a third turn.

$$2 \times 23 + 2 = 48$$

Will it be the same equation if the three children absent return tomorrow?

Having groaned that they couldn't move, the children came to the decision that frogs needed room to move and swim. Several requested an 'open' space into which they could move. They found that not even half our number could stretch out and swim without constantly colliding. In any spare time the children kept returning and trying to 'swim freely' around the pool to establish how many frogs would be able to live in our pond. From this came the suggestion of volume and depth of the pond. They wouldn't all be at the same depth and, indeed, in the pond at the same time.

Some frogs were ordered to sit on the bank to allow room for others. How many could sit around the edge, or perimeter?

Soon the children were measuring the perimeter of everything. They were subtracting and adding numbers to the measurement gained, depending on the suitability of the edge for the frogs to sit. Some shapes demanded new strategies to measure such odd shapes.

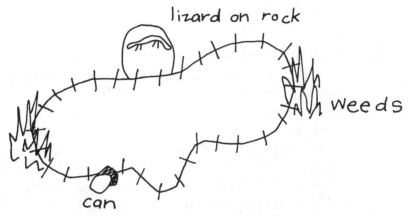

Caitlin said, 'My pond measured 31 pop sticks around. One frog could fit on each stick. But there was an old rusty can so the frogs didn't want to sit near that. So $31 - 3 = 28$ spaces for frogs. Then there were two big, bushy parts where the ducks were — and they eat frogs so $28 - 2 \times 3 = 22$. On the other side was a big rough rock with a lizard sunbaking on it'.

At this point Caitlin sought help, as her picture of the rock was placed unevenly on her recording. It was taking up one and two half spaces.

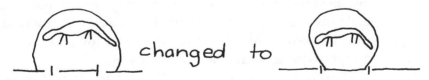

She listened to my own and other children's explanations, still wasn't confident in her own mind and so adjusted her drawing of the rock to relieve the problem of adding halves. She then wrote $22 - 1 = 21$ spaces for frogs. This indicated to me that she was unsure of adding parts as drawn originally: ½ + 1 + ½.

The following day I set a group of children, including Caitlin, a problem involving the fraction aspect with which she had shown some reluctance through lack of experience and understanding.

'You could sit two frogs instead of one on each of your sticks', interceded Brett. He had used a smaller lid as his measure.

Caitlin then went on happily to explore that possibility, which would involve doubling all her previous calculations.

'My frogs are too fat', said Curtis. (He had also used a pop-stick measure and wasn't too sure about Caitlin's enthusiasm for doubling her numbers.) So I provided his next challenge:

'Your frogs have eaten so much they need two pop sticks to sit on.' Curtis readily went off to halve his numbers. He liked the challenge of fat frogs!

Swimming, sitting, gliding

The children also made paper cut-outs of frogs sitting, swimming and gliding. They spent time placing these on the pond in various combinations:

3 gliding	+ 4 sitting	+ 2 swimming	= 9
3 swimming	+ 4 sitting	+ 2 gliding	= 9
7 sitting	+ 4 swimming	+ 1 gliding	= 12

The children had agreed that the frogs gliding took up approximately the same space as those swimming. How then could twelve frogs fit in the pool?

'Easy', said Ben. 'Four are sitting in the pond and the others are right at the edge. They've got their toes in.'

'Some frogs could sit on top of the water while others swam, if we had lily-pads', said Tessa.

How many lily-pads could cover our pond?

This was excellent reinforcement as well as a new source of a learning situation on area.

Can you play leapfrog?

We measured how far we could all leap, establishing starting points and finishing points. We measured from where our toes started to where they finished. From this came the need for an exact measure: a tape showing metres and centimetres.

Starting with jumping from lily-pad to lily-pad to see who could jump the most before collapsing, Fiona decided to leap over two at a time. 'That way I won't get as tired, and I'll jump more!' This started lots of pattern work and counting by 2s, 3s and 4s.

Then the problem-solving question: Starting on the first lily-pad and jumping over two at each jump, Fiona jumped four times. How many lily-pads did she need?

'That's stand on one, over two...that's three', said Jessie. A number of children agreed.

'No it's not', said Barbara. 'It's 13. Look.' She explained her answer using our 'lily-pads':

one to start and   4 × 3

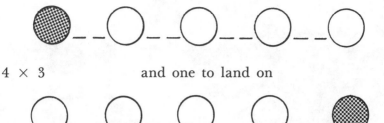

4 × 3   and one to land on

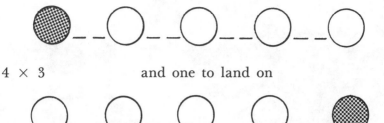

Shortly afterward Rhett said, 'I could jump backwards, too. Watch me.'

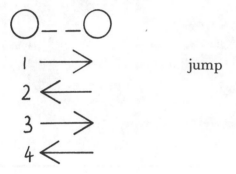

jump

'I only needed four lily-pads.'

We then explored lots of other combinations and possibilities, but always needed the extra lily-pad to land on.

'What if we could jump in a circle?' said Caitlin.

We decided to leave that for the butterflies!

My frog's different

The children all made frogs from drink cartons and plastic cake containers. They used these constantly in place of counters for classification according to size, colour, mouth shape, etc.

In the making of these models, the children had to select and adjust their carton to make either a small, short frog, a tall, thin frog, a short, fat frog or a tall, fat frog. When we finished there were a number of variations besides the four listed. We discussed the reasons for this — cut too short or too long, a different brand of container, etc. — and were able to sequence them in height and size.

When placing the paper eye circles inside the plastic, the children discovered another aspect.

'My frog's looking the other way.'

'Mine's looking up.'

'Where's yours looking?'

By changing the positioning of the 'eyeball' we had changed the direction of where the frog was looking.

Using these frogs the children were constantly verbalising, writing and recording mathematical stories, using a combination of creative story-writing techniques, ordinary and mathematical language, and written numbers and equations. The rearrangement, substitution and equivalence of numbers were extensively discussed and debated.

I only had to listen and I knew the children's strengths and weaknesses. Some I approached as a group learning situation, others as a class or individual learning situation.

Tadpoles

A small group of children made peg tadpoles, which gave rise to the question:

'How big or long should we make the body in proportion to the tail?'

For this activity we went back to our live tadpoles. They also provided many problem-solving activities. How many legs on ten tadpoles? Each week or day, a different answer. We kept a diary of tadpole changes and activities. The passage of time was made meaningful to the children.

The balance scales looked like two ponds so we were able to include lots of balance and weight activities as well as size, shape, etc.

Storytime frog problems

The children loved to come into our 'classroom pond' and seek out a new problem. What is happening at the pond today?

I would often write a story which they could use as a language activity for reading and creative writing, or as an art activity, and which involved mathematical concepts. The children often wrote similar stories to share with the class and we set these up in display areas. Often these were used as a particular group's work for the day.

Sam the Snake was silently gliding across the pond.
He could see fat frogs resting on lilypads .. EVERYWHERE
Yum, yum!)
If he were very sneaky he thought he could eat five for
breakfast, five for lunch, then ten for tea. Then maybe
the same the next day.
But a kingfisher was sitting up in the old gum tree.
He wondered if he could open and shut his beak quickly
enough to catch two frogs at a time. Maybe he could swoop
down three times.
Twenty frogs croaked happily.   What happened?

Leah made a large box mural for the story about the snake and the kingfisher. She had a bush setting of trees, hills and sky at the back, then in the foreground the pond, snake, frogs, gum tree and kingfisher. She also added lots of other details.

She wrote a creative story imagining she was the snake and gave her thoughts before, during and after the attack.

The following day she wrote as an observer watching the kingfisher and frogs.

During this time she also proposed many alternative solutions to the mathematical problem by changing the time of day the kingfisher was at the pond. Another child decided catching the two frogs at once hurt the kingfisher's beak and so he gave up and flew away. Another allowed him to swoop down five times while the snake was still sunbaking. The snake went without his meal. This led to my next story.

There were sixteen frogs in a pond.

An old tortoise was sitting on a rock nearby, watching them.

But he had a sore mouth. One side was very swollen, so when

he snapped his mouth he always caught an uneven number

of frogs.

After three snaps his mouth was too sore to continue.

How many frogs could he eat?   What might have happened?

Using a large packet of lolly frogs Nolan was creating his own maths story. The grade was currently attending weekly swimming lessons and the circus was coming to town the following week. So Nolan's story evolved.

They all thought they would go for a swim at the Leisure Centre.
They stayed too late and they didn't even pay their entrance
fee. Clown said he would take them away. They could help him
with his circus act.
So we built him a unifix trailer.
It was nine blocks long and we put four blocks each end for
the width.

$$2 \times 9 + 2 \times 4$$

Guess how many frogs he fitted in his trailer?

When I helped the clown he fitted fifteen frogs in his trailer.

We drove backwards and forwards to the circus ten times.

All those frogs!!

10 x 15 ?

The following day I added to Nolan's story!

He had to build lots of cages to keep them in, because
the Leisure Centre DIDN'T WANT THEM BACK !!!!!

He could build small cages which would hold ten frogs

and big cages which could hold twenty frogs.

WHAT WOULD HE BUILD ?   There are lots of answers

  In the photo Nolan, Adam and Ben are working out the many answers
to Nolan's problem of putting 150 frogs in large cages holding twenty
and small cages holding ten. During this activity they were constantly
sorting into bundles of ten, adding and multiplying, which formed

the basis for later work in place value. They were also reinforcing their earlier work of perimeter and area.

Nolan became so involved that he brought frog cartoons from home. For a child who was very confident with mathematics, but hesitant and far less confident with reading, here was a breakthrough. He was reading while happily concentrating on his maths.

What happens to illegally parked frogs. They get toad away.

Flowers

In a smiliar manner to 'Frogs' you may like to develop the theme of 'Flowers' or 'In the Garden'. Start with a nature walk in the school garden or buy a bunch of fresh flowers. The children also love making trees and flowers to decorate the room for spring or autumn.

These are some of the areas I found interesting to develop.

1 Look at the number of petals on the flowers. Make some of your own and discover the shape differences and number patterns.

EXAMPLE

3×6 round petals $+ 3 \times 6$ thin petals
or 6 flowers with 6 petals $= 6 \times 6$

2 How many leaves are there on each branch or stem?

3 Compare the shape, size and thickness of leaves.

4 Area: Where do the leaves fall?

How far are they blown?

Which direction would the wind be blowing?

See how many trees shed their leaves in a defined area.

5 Weight: Find the number and weight of leaves collected in one week over one square metre. Try this at different times of the year.

6 Make a tree using a variety of paper strips. Have the children describe which strips to use and where to place them to make an identical tree or one in the reverse shape.

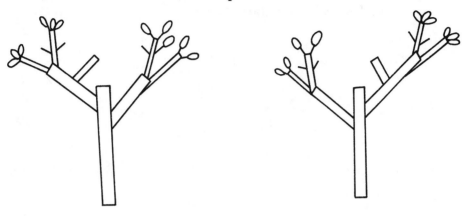

Did your tree end up the same?
If not, how did it differ?

At the goldfields

You might like to brainstorm ideas for a mathematical theme on 'The Goldfields'.

Here are a few suggestions to start you on your way.

1 How large is the area to be mined?

2 Depth of the mines. You might compare these to open-cut and diamond mines.

3 The weight of gold. While rocks are not anywhere near as heavy as gold, it is fun to spray-paint lots of rocks gold and have the children weigh and order them, find two to equal one, etc.

4 The amount of gold found in the quartz. Older children could explore percentage and ratio.

5 Map reading and orienteering skills to find the goldfields.

100 years ago

Compare our life today with that of settlers 100 years ago. Some activities which you might like to start with are:

1 What would you need to order in supplies for one month? You must consider the lifestyle of the time. Would you need eggs and butter? What refrigeration was available? Consider the weight of the goods you purchase. Can you carry them? Might you need to plan for the months ahead, e.g. seed for sowing, wool or material for clothing, nails for building, etc.

2 What are your water resources like?

Study how much water we use personally each day, compared with what we need. Should we conserve water today? Why? Look at rainfall. Read your home water meter to determine how much water a washing machine or dishwasher uses.

3 How long does a candle take to burn? Compare this with electricity. Now add some more ideas that you and the children have thought of. How will you start them?

THE ZOO

A visit to a zoo, a wildlife sanctuary or a fauna park is an experience that should be, and in most instances is, often repeated. With each visit we gain new insights into the world of animals and their natural or artificial environments.

I have pursued the following activities with primary age children following excursions to the zoo or in conjunction with general studies discussions, literature, creative play, etc.

Whether it be a zoo or a wildlife sanctuary, all the activities can easily be adapted to suit the animals or conditions experienced by your own group of children.

Identification and classification of zoo animals is virtually a reflex action by children when presented with toy animals. Depending on the actual zoo visited they may isolate some animals as pets. Areas of classification could be size, body covering, texture, nocturnal or diurnal, country of origin, fast or slow moving, reptiles, mammals, marsupials, herbivorous, carnivorous or omnivorous. Older children may combine several of these classifications and may like to research some of the more unusual animals. Young children should be encouraged to classify by new characteristics, e.g. nocturnal, herbivorous, after the initial sorting activities. During the course of the children's sorting and classifying it is interesting to include a fieldmouse or a worm. Would this be found in the zoo? This enlarges the concept of the word 'zoo'. Its boundaries are far more extensive than the exhibiting areas.

During the last few years zoological gardens everywhere have redesigned and built many of their enclosures in an effort to re-create the natural habitat of the animals. A study of this area lends itself to the children studying comparative sizes of animals and similar and common habitats.

Our own zoo

As a starting point the class and I sat together with six plastic lions, fifteen monkeys, three elephants, four polar bears, seven snakes and three seals. We decided these animals were being sent across the world to us and we needed to start building our zoo at once. What would we need?

The children collected:

fences — pop sticks

grass — cardboard squares to indicate the grassed areas

trees — cotton reels with straws, plasticene base with sticks, inter-locking daisy shapes

water — aerosol-can lids as drinking troughs, blue squares to be assembled as pool or creek

cages — boxes turned side on, Lego, etc.

gates — blocks and scraps of mesh

sleeping quarters — boxes, stones to build a cave, building blocks.

There was lots of discussion, both positive and negative, but always with the goal of making our animals comfortable. I have always insisted our criticism be constructive.

When Samuel placed fifteen monkeys on one fenced-in grass square and Katie had used twenty squares for two of her three elephants, the children's discussion enabled me to assess their undertsanding of the area needed for each animal.

Samuel was happy as he had trees in his enclosure that the monkeys could climb. Paul was most adamant: 'They need to run and jump and swing'.

Samuel 'They're only little.'

Paul 'They move a lot though.'

Katie 'They probably wouldn't be good trees all growing together like that. You need big and little trees—all sizes.'

Samuel 'I could use some of your space then.' (All the squares had been used by this time.)

Katie 'I've still got another elephant yet. It gets cross and fights so I was going to make it another enclosure.' (Katie really wanted lots of ground space for her elephants and wasn't prepared to concede any. She had had a quick look at other animals' spaces and realised some of them could concede space easily.)

Paul 'If you used Katie's elephant enclosure your monkeys could climb the trees and jump out over the wall.' (He started to move the trees to a more central location.)

With this Samuel realised his need for a modification to his enclosure as well as the need to negotiate with someone else to relinquish ground space. Katie set about redesigning her grass lay-out to gain extra space, while providing a separating gate for her elephant. He was to rejoin the others at a later date. (Later in the day she wrote a creative story about her elephants fighting.)

At the same time Claire and Rhys were building the lions' enclosure. They had immediately selected strong posts and mesh. Lions wouldn't like a dark enclosure. They like to sit out in the sun. They also tried various ways of arranging their twenty-eight grass squares. They selected this number then checked to see how many they had compared with Katie and her three elephants. They appeared satisfied with the comparison.

They laid them out in a 4 x 7 pattern and immediately started re-organising them.

Claire   'Lions run really fast, don't they.'

Rhys   (as he moved squares) 'We'd better make this space a bit longer.'

Claire   'They'd get sick of running backwards and forwards though. Let's give them a corner to get out of the way.'

Claire and Rhys both made corners.

How do we calculate area?

I asked how many squares Claire and Rhys had used.

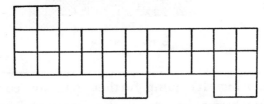

To recheck their twenty-eight squares they added by 2s along the centre, then the protruding squares — again by 2s.

'How many 2s have you?'

They then became interested in all the different number patterns they could see emerging and explained them to me. They went on to record their work for all to share. (See page 84.)

This exercise came spontaneously from the children's discussion, provided a sharing of ideas and showed their knowledge of mental and written computations.

They then resumed building their lions' enclosure. While making a den out of rocks they discovered balance, height, shape and placement. 'Not too close to the netting or they might leap up and scramble over', said Rhys. They then made the base wall a little higher. Claire measured her lion against the actual blocks as she visually determined how far it could jump to reach the wire.

I interrupted to ask 'How tall would a real lion be, Claire?'

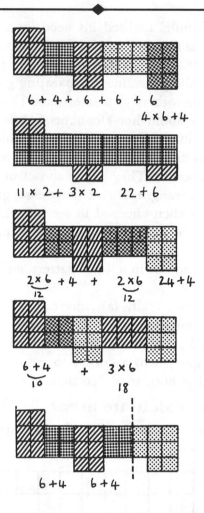

6 + 4 + 6 + 6 + 6

4 × 6 + 4

11 × 2 + 3 × 2   22 + 6

2 × 6 + 4 + 2 × 6   24 + 4
—————   —————
  12   12

6 + 4 + 3 × 6
————   18
 10

6 + 4   6 + 4

'Pretty big. It'd jump further than you could', she replied.

At lunchtime she went to the library and found how big lions are. She measured and marked the length and height of an African lion on our back wall. This led to the class seeking various resources to find the height of a giraffe, the length of a python, the height — and weight — of an elephant, etc.

Could a giraffe stand up in our classroom?

Could an elephant fit through the door?

We used wildlife books, the *Guinness Book of Records*, the local vet and telephoned the zoo's Education Service to compare record heights with the animals currently at the zoo.

'If they are that big they must eat HEAPS!' exclaimed Joshua. And our maths was channelled in yet another direction.

What food would a zoo need?

We decided to order food for our animals.

What variety of food would we need? Nuts, hay, lucerne, fresh leaves, meat (alive or slaughtered?), vegetables and fruit. The task was astronomical, so we limited our variety and number of animals.

Would they eat the same every day?

Would their eating habits change during the year, e.g. snakes hibernating during colder months?

How often would the food be delivered?

Again estimation was widely used and we sought further assistance from the zoo's Education Service and from a wildlife sanctuary.

In the higher primary levels an excellent activity is to estimate, then ascertain exactly, the cost of feeding one or more of the animals. Comparisons can be made between different zoo animals and the cost compared with that of our pets at home. Why are some foods dearer than others?

At the same time we all enjoyed writing about the escapades of the animals. The children loved creating scary, frightening, exciting and especially mischievous stories.

We wrote lots of 'maths stories'. These varied in focus from vocabulary describing position, time, etc., to number computations. Sometimes I wrote the story and included problems to solve. I used these stories as class problem-solving activities and as extension or revision work for targeted groups of children. My writing also stimulated the children to write their own stories and problems. Many times the stories developed further after a child or I added 'But what if...?'

Activity questions such as these
were used in many ways:
. class problem solving exercises
. extension work for early finishers
. they stimulated children to create
  their own problems for the grade
. some children needed to be guided
  in eliciting pertinent facts e.g.
  (They had seven) (2kg. buckets)

Unfortunately the elephant stood on the vet's
calculator whilst he was attending to his
sore foot, yesterday. Can you assist him?

He needs to make up some drops for the lion's
infected eyes, and isn't sure how much he'll
need.
The lion should have four drops in each eye
early morning, midday, late afternoon and
at night. He will require these for five days
then only three times a day for another two
days.

If he could get five drops from each ml.
(millilitre), how much should he bottle?

When the keeper went to his food store
he got a nasty shock. The monkeys had
escaped and run riot!

If five bananas weigh 1 kg, and they ate
7½ kg, how many bananas did they eat?

They had seven, 2kg buckets of mixed nuts.
they ate half and threw the remainder
at each other. 200 nuts weigh 1kg.
If there were nine monkeys, how many
nuts did they each eat?

Next they cut the fruit into halves.
They thought they were very clever!
The keeper found 26 orange halves and
42 apple halves in one bucket. In another,
he found 12 apple quarters and fifteen
orange thirds.
How much fruit had they ruined?

The children were given the equation below and asked to create their own story about any of the 'Big Cats'. They responded with a diversity of situations. The stories were typed from their verbal explanations and compiled into an experience book.

Similar books were made with 'monkeys', 'butterflies', etc.

There were two tigresses walking along near the river. It was a very hot day and they wanted a drink and a swim. They each had three cubs. They brought them along so they could teach them to swim.
Oh, what a terrible day!! The crocodiles came gliding quietly up and snapped up four of the cubs.

Claire B.

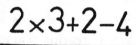

$$2 \times 3 + 2 - 4$$

The three tigers were out enjoying the hot afternoon sun. But very soon they were disturbed by three roly-poly cubs. They kept climbing all over them and biting their ears. They wanted the tigers to play with them. AND THEN...

when the tigers saw two more cubs coming over to play they started to growl. Why couldn't those cubs leave them in peace?
Tails swishing they got up and went over to their cage. Now they could rest. One very tired little cub curled up and went to sleep with them too.

A problem zoo in our room

Another grade was participating with us in our zoo theme. They made their classroom into a zoo. They placed toy animals in their enclosures — tables, chairs, blocks, etc. The enclosures were arranged in alphabetical order according to the animal's name. (There are a variety of ways you might like to arrange the enclosures.)

In each enclosure there was an odd number of animals. The number in each enclosure increased by two as you moved from one enclosure to the next: in the first enclosure was one animal, in the next three and so on.

The following animals were in the zoo — kangaroo, Tasmanian devil, possum, echidna, pelican, koala, wombat, emu, meerkat, squirrel, cassowary and platypus.

- How many enclosures were there?
- What animals, and how many, were in the sixth, ninth and third-last enclosures?

- How many birds were in the classroom zoo?
- Name the non-Australian animals. How many were there altogether in this zoo?
- Were there more koalas or kangaroos?
- How many platypuses were there? Would you expect to see so many at a real zoo?
- Which animal enclosure had the largest number of animals? How many animals were there?
- Write the names of the mother animals who would have a pouch.

An open-ended problem-solving situation arises if you do not stipulate that the first enclosure has only one animal. Alternatively, you could double the number of animals as you progressed. You can easily structure the situation in your story to suit the mathematical concept you wish to pursue.

Some children made a large box construction and paper maché crocodile. Comparisons and measuring strategies were discussed during its construction. Then they created a story out in 'crocodile country'. The crocodile ate many creatures but some escaped; he had to submerge and remain hidden while hunters searched for him, and he was joined by other crocodiles in the hunt for food.

Lots of fun, lots of mathematics — explanations, clarification, revision and extension.

While some six year olds were setting out their animals, there was discussion concerning numbers, placement of the animals, size of paddocks and many other possible variations. They decided to record some of their ideas by providing the relevant equations.

What shape will I make it?

A group of children (six and seven year olds) all started with twenty-four logs each. They were asked to make an enclosure for their animals. I had envisaged enclosures of 2×12, 12×2, 4×6, 6×4, 3×8 and 8×3. Unexpectedly, not one child constructed any of the above. I had sought to show them the relationship between 3×8 and 8×3, etc., but they certainly went much further than that.

'We wouldn't want it just sort of square or a rectangle', said Helen. 'That wouldn't be any good for the animals.'

Was my lesson lost? Certainly not. The children had extended the lesson to include the concept of area. Which enclosure had the most space?

They decided to measure the area inside their fences using uniform-sized plastic squares. They then asked to record their results for later reference and so they could explore and compare further possibilities. They moved sections of fencing to extend or reduce the area.

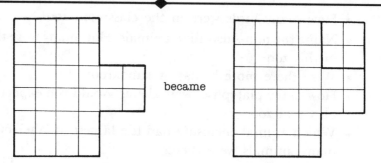

became

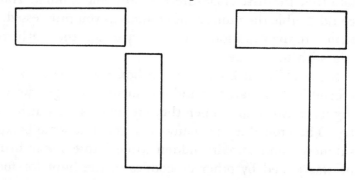

While recording, they also discovered the need for the strips to be exactly the same length and to place the corners exactly.

Should they meet... or overlap?

The children discussed the relative strengths of each arrangement. If they strengthened their walls in this way did it affect the area? What happened to the measurement of the perimeter? If you were ordering supplies, what allowances might you need to make? Older children could explore these possibilities in far more depth.

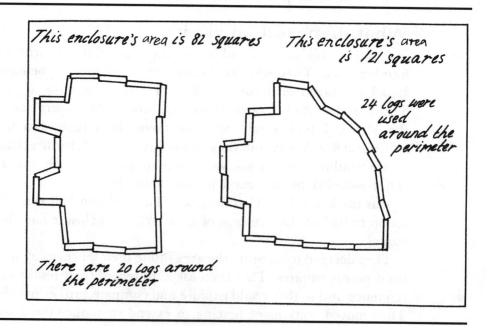

This enclosure's area is 82 squares

This enclosure's area is 121 squares

24 logs were used around the perimeter

There are 20 logs around the perimeter

A 'mistake' became positive when interest focused on Paul's enclosure of twenty logs and an area of eighty-two squares, as opposed to Brent's enclosure of more logs (twenty-four) and less area (sixty-seven squares). At this stage I suggested they both make rectangular shapes then compare their respective 'possible' areas.

(When they initially counted their 'square' areas they had actually focused on my original intention of showing $8 \times 3 = 3 \times 8$, etc.) Several children tried comparing their enclosures in the same way.

'Well, it depends on what you want', said Katie.

'What if you needed a higher wall?' asked Paul.

The possibilities of extending into other mathematical areas were endless.

THE
FARAWAY TREE

This theme started when the children chose the book *The Enchanted Wood* from one of several presented to be read as a literature appreciation serial.

They had had little or no experience with fantasy previously at the school, and most were at the stage of wobbly teeth and discussing the 'Tooth Fairy' avidly. The Faraway Tree theme therefore provided a new avenue of interest — one in which the children's creativity could be challenged — and certainly related to their immediate world.

A further social outcome of this theme was the development of a sense of proportion between reality and fantasy. While fully understanding 'reality', they used it as a starting point or a point of comparison and thoroughly enjoyed spreading their wings with fantasy.

Discussing the Faraway Tree itself led to exploring the school grounds and the adjacent vacant land. Which of the trees could be the Faraway Tree? We considered height, width, shape, size and texture of the trunk, the number of branches, whether they were strong enough and the apparent age of the trees.

This area of study alone can be developed further in the fields of sorting, classification, etc. With older children the study of leaf growth and fall, comparing a deciduous tree to an evergreen, leads to some interesting speculations, revelations and very extensive mathematical calculations. Start with specifying one square metre of ground and see how many leaves fall in one day. Alternatively, choose an isolated deciduous tree and track how far, and in what direction, its leaves travel on different days.

An example of the degree to which simple observations or assumptions can lead to very complex mathematical calculations is Schleiger's study to ascertain whether leaf fall beneath a tree is random, regular or clumped. (See References.)

Our own Faraway Tree

The children wished they had their own Faraway Tree.

What to use for a huge tree trunk?

We considered boxes and cardboard tubes. Hunting in a storage area under the school we found a roll of chicken wire. Initially considering a straight cylindrical shape, to gain height and stability we ended with a conical shape with quite a wide base. Wanting a section to sit inside the tree led to the base being opened out to form a wide spiral with an internal support and a light to see by.

The measuring, estimating, trial and error that the children attempted and persevered with was far beyond what I would previously have expected or attempted with this group of seven and eight year olds.

Our art and mathematical activities were inseparable at this stage. Covering the trunk of the tree was easy. Pieces of brown paper were torn hurriedly from a large roll and everybody pasted.

While this was a comparatively short exercise, the mathematical concepts covered were extensive. The children discussed, observed and measured:

- Whose paper was the biggest, longest, widest, thinnest, almost square, rectangular or triangular?
- How many pieces could be covered before the paste needed refilling?
- How many scoops of paste to a margarine container?
- The need for ensuring that the perimeter as well as the middle of the paper was well pasted.
- The need to overlap the paper as it went on the wire frame and the shape most suitable to fill a particular space.

Most of these concepts were discussed informally and needed constant rethinking as more pieces were required.

We had decided that the tree needed several different types of branches but that we would need to work in groups on each area to produce the effect we wanted.

We had a wide range of scrap materials. In groups the children decided on their pattern or style of work and chose suitable materials. Some chose the materials first, then discovered how they could use them.

Group 1 chose popcorn and threaded it in a colour pattern of their own choice, considering as they did so: length of threading wool, colour of the popcorn pattern, size and shape of the popcorn, how many threaded, how many in a handful, how many broken in half, how much 'disappeared'. (Every time they threaded ten they could eat one piece.) Counting skills, value relationships and size were quickly mastered.

Group 2 chose giant flowers made from milk cartons cut in half and covered with a colour pattern of fringed paper which involved: measuring the paper to cover the carton, placing the carton correctly and cutting to the corners, folding paper squares in four to make strips, then equal-distance fringing.

Group 3 chose the large branch of a gum tree, and selecting one of the smaller branches each, they painted leaves with their favourite colour, deciding as they did so: how many leaves on each branch, placement along the stem, size of the leaves, how many yellow, etc., and using positional language — above, below, underneath, etc.

Group 4 made large green leaves from a variety of paper textures and bunched them together in fours and fives. This led to grouping, adding and multiplying.

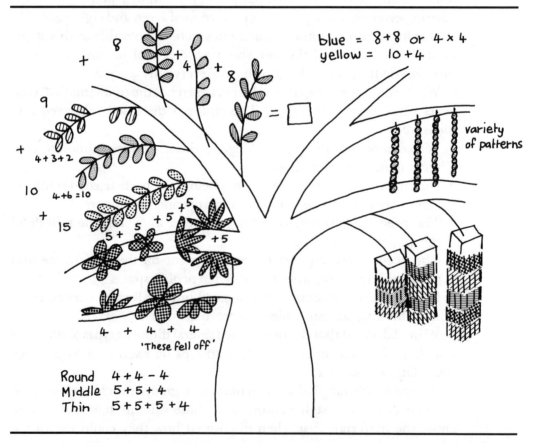

There were so many ideas about the land at the top of the tree that we decided to list them all during a brainstorming session. Following a discussion as to how these would be developed, we voted for our three favourite lands. For example, the Land of Chomp was suggested because we were interested in the Tooth Fairy and because the regional dental van was scheduled to visit with its large set of dentures and toothbrush.

We were unable to follow up many of the ideas as a class, but the children later wrote maths stories about them and created problem-solving activities for themselves and for others to see and share.

The 'Land of Chomp' title caused us to wonder who could take the largest bite, or chomp! We all brought an apple for lunch the following day to investigate and compare size, type and shapes of apples, who had the biggest, smallest, same-sized bite, and how many bites in an apple. When the children had eaten their apples we recorded how many bites taken.

1	child	with	7	bites or		7
6	children	with	8	bites	6×8	$8+8+8+8+8+8$
4	children	with	9	bites	4×9	$9+9+9+9$
5	children	with	12	bites	5×12	$12+12+12+12+12$
7	children	with	13	bites	7×13	$13+13+13+13+13+13+13$
					$=?$	

This activity led to a giant from the Land of Giants being left behind at the top of the tree. He'd taken an enormous bite. How big would his mouth be?

A group of nine year old children decided to make huge giant's teeth. They discussed the different sizes of teeth — front compared to molars — and made the giant's teeth one hundred times as large as their own. The mouth was enormous! Another group made a huge mouth, then tried to work out how big the giant would be. The size and proportion concepts shown by the children were very revealing of the maturity levels reached.

I wrote a story for the children.

Up in the 'Land of Chomp' — that's where everything about teeth is to be found — the Tooth Fairy had a problem. One of the giant's children had a loose tooth and when she went to collect it she was very surprised. Such big teeth would be very useful for building, but oh, it was such a bad tooth!

Didn't the Giant family use their toothbrushes?

So the Tooth Fairy hid in their bathroom the next morning. They had hundreds of toothbrushes, and the strange ways they tried using them! The giant kept dropping his. The brushes were just too small. She would need to make giant sized brushes.

Whatever would she use?

We discussed lots of possibilities until a child suggested prickles. We had to consider what was long, would be plentiful enough, not too brittle, uniform in size, etc. Together we continued discussing and writing the story.

> The following day the Tooth Fairy was discussing her problem with the folk from the Faraway Tree. But soon they all became angry. The naughty pixie kept poking and jabbing them with a long prickle.
>
> 'What a nuisance. I wish he'd do something nice', growled Mr Watzisname.
>
> Suddenly the Tooth Fairy knew what to use for bristles. That's right. The big, long prickles that had fallen to the ground from the bush that grew near the bottom of the hill. His name was Peter Prickle Bush.

I asked the children to be a prickle bush and consider how many prickles they would give. This varied, but most agreed they would probably only lose one at a time, as we never see this type of bush without its prickles. The bush needs them to keep animals away.

> Peter Prickle Bush agreed to give the Tooth Fairy a prickle from each of his eight branches, every Friday. She was very pleased. That made one row of bristles for the giant's toothbrush. Each week she had another row.
>
> But oh dear! Peter Prickle Bush had given her lots of prickles — sixty-four when they counted — but now he had no more loose ones.
>
> Luckily the Tooth Fairy has lots of friends.

Using a large polystyrene rectangle and straws, we made the toothbrush.

When we ran out of green straws the shape of the toothbrush wasn't complete. One of the children suggested the Tooth Fairy could find another sort of prickle bush.

'What about rose thorns', said Fiona. 'They are sort of hooked and could clean around the corners of the giant's big teeth.'

'But he'd have trouble rubbing the brush backwards and forwards', said Josh.

'The top of a pineapple's prickly', said Andy. So the Tooth Fairy would use the spiky leaves to be found at the top of a pineapple. We decided it must be summer.

As we added to our story each day we also added to our problem-solving card.

- How many prickles did the branches on Peter Prickle Bush give the Tooth Fairy each week?
- How many rows would she have
  - in a fortnight
  - in a month?
- How many rows did she make before Peter Prickle Bush ran out of prickles?

- When she used the pineapple leaves, how many leaves went across each row?
- For how many weeks did Pamela Pineapple give the Tooth Fairy leaves?
- How many weeks did it take to make the toothbrush?

> When the Tooth Fairy had put in half the prickles Peter Prickle Bush had given her she realised each prickle took two minutes to fix and glue.
>   How long had it taken?
>   Then along came a cheery woodpecker.
>   He drilled the holes and the rest only took half the time.
>   How long did it take to make the giant's toothbrush?

We introduced the woodpecker to the story at this time, as we had just discovered a quicker method of placing the straws in the polystyrene and had wondered which animal could make holes quickly. Our story continued.

> Over the next two weeks Pamela Pineapple gave her enough spiky leaves to make another row on each side.
>   Then she gave enough in the following weeks to make a top row and a bottom row.
>   The toothbrush was finished at last!
>   The giant was delighted and the Tooth Fairy promised him another one at the same time next year.

During this part of the theme we were involved in:
- the use of a calendar
- the number of days in a week, month, etc.
- the date in eight weeks time
- the minutes in one hour
- addition, multiplication and subtraction, particularly when counting the toothbrush 'prickles'.

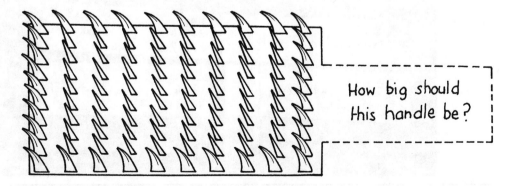

How big should this handle be?

Prickles from Peter Prickle Bush

$8+8+8+8+8+8+8+8=64$

$8\times8=64$

Pamela Pineapple's leaves

$8+8=16$ (sides)

$10\ \ +\ 2\times10\ \ \ \ \ =30$

t o p + bottom rows

The toothbrush showed us our eight and ten multiplication tables. These were soon well known.

Several children conducted their own survey on the colour and brand of the class's toothbrushes and graphed the results.

At this stage, although most children were still interested in continuing 'Toothbrush maths', I felt that most of the possible areas had been covered and they would benefit more from a new input.

Silky and Saucepan

As our serial of 'The Faraway Tree' progressed, the children related closely to Silky and Saucepan, who both lived in the tree.

We had a lively activity when the children tried fitting saucepans on their own heads. How big would Saucepan's saucepan be if he was small enough to live in a tree? How big would a tree need to be if we lived in it? (For ten and eleven year old children, Jean George's *My Side of the Mountain* tells of a boy's survival in the Catskill Mountains in May. A delightful and poignant story, it tells of the hardships and delights of seeking shelter, food gathering and hunting, furniture making, the changing weather and seasons, animal life, and so on. A wonderful variety of mathematical ideas to explore.)

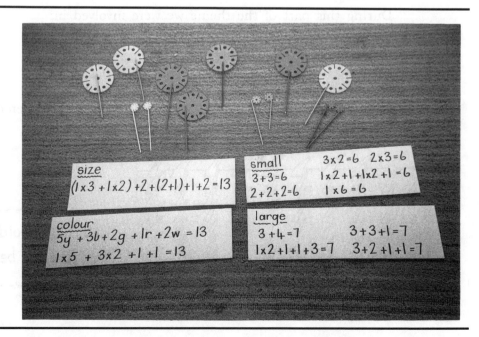

Here is Silky's window.

Can you colour the flowers in her window pots? In the lefthand one she has blue + yellow + yellow + pink + red.

In the right hand pot she has small blue and pink and large red and yellow flowers.

Which colours make these equations?

$3 + 2 + 1 + 1 + 2 = 9$

$3 \times 2 + 1 + 1 + 1 = 9$

$6 L + 2s + 1s = 9$

* Colour in the flowers on the curtains. Can you make up your own equations?

We made Silky's window and put it on our tree. Then we worked out where all the characters lived in the tree in relation to each other.

Who was always getting wet from Dame Washalot's water?

Would he or she have to live above or below Dame Washalot?

At the bottom of the tree we left a directory of how to reach each tenant's doorway.

We made flower pots in front of Silky's window and the children quickly commented on the number, colour and size of the flowers.

Recording these observations came easily when we reproduced our tiny flower beds with large manipulative equipment.

The children followed this class activity by making a flower design for Silky to plant for the following spring. When would she need to plant the bulbs and the seedlings? All at the same time?

Initially I restricted the colours by only providing a choice of four.

There was still the choice of large and small, any position and number.

Since working further with the thematic approach, I find most children do this themselves as they develop a concept of the end result they wish to achieve. They realise a mass of colours, shapes, sizes, etc., can in itself be restricting. Reducing the variables initially helps children and the teacher to gain confidence in the thematic approach.

During the theme the children had been writing letters to the 'Faraway Folk' and had often received an answer as well as signs or messages left out, e.g. 'Back in ten minutes', 'Meet me at Dame Washalot's'.

One morning a jar of tiny home-made toffees 'mysteriously' appeared at the bottom of the tree and excitement and speculation built up until a note arrived after the lunch recess.

Hello School Kids,

   What a surprise I got when I arrived home for lunch today. A big jar of toffees from Bessie. Did you see them? Silky said they came to visit and I was out. I'm glad you watched my toffees or the Naughty Pixie might have hidden them — or eaten them! It is such a lovely big jar with so many toffees — and so crunchy, sticky and gooey. I have two in my mouth at the moment. Would you all like to taste one, seeing you looked after my jar?
I was away for the last two nights staying with my gnome friends at the other end of the Enchanted Wood. Misty wasn't feeling well — he had a sore throat — so I took him some toffees to suck. It was lovely and warm there at night as they cuddle up with the squirrels in the hollow in the tree.
What are the strange things in your room?
Did they escape from one of the lands at the top of the tree? Are they dangerous or friendly?
I have to go out again today, but maybe you could leave a note in my letterbox.
Don't forget, I'll let you try one of my toffees.
Good-bye for now,
Moonface

What can you do with a jar of toffees?
- count them
- share them
- compare the number of hundreds and thousands on them
  — more, less, colours
- time taken to melt in your mouth
- consideration of quantity, sharing for broken or 'stuck' toffees
- if we eat one each a day, how long will they last?
- make toffees yourselves — ingredients, cooking, cooling
- enjoy eating them!

Of course we had a lovely time with the toffees and wrote a quick reply. Reading, writing and mathematics were all one.

```
The Yellow Door
The Faraway Tree
Early Friday Morning

Dear School Kids,
   I'm glad you enjoyed the toffees. I certainly did. I think I'll have two
more after breakfast — I always have one crumpet cut into sixths. Moon-
face eats one piece, the two squirrels from the branch opposite share
one piece and save another section for tea. I eat two pieces and I usually
have an early morning visitor who is quite eager to eat the rest.
I'd like to know how Silky makes Pop Biscuits, too. But she doesn't tell
anyone her secret recipe. We all think it must be magic.
I'm glad your creatures are friendly.
Oh, here comes Watzisname. I guess he'll eat the rest of the crumpet
and have a cup of tea. I must hurry. I have a busy market day.
Moonface
```

This letter generated far more activity by the children than I ever anticipated. They were very busy learning, as they had fun cutting and sharing make-believe crumpets and writing stories about how many visitors came to Moonface's the next morning for 'tea and crumpets' and how they shared and divided them.

The children also brought along their favourite biscuit recipe and we compared the ingredients, the quantities, types and baking temperatures. These we were able to graph and then discover relevant information. For example, which are the quickest to make? Which recipe makes the most? Why? If I double the mixture to make the same amount as the other recipe will the cooking time alter?

Several mothers came one day to help us bake our favourite recipes.

Measurement, time, addition, subtraction, multiplication and division became very important and relevant to all.

I had left a basket of paper 'clothing' under our Faraway Tree. The children pegged out the clothes, matching sock patterns, mitten sizes, etc. They wrote number stories to hang on the line. Two big pairs of mittens and three big pairs of socks

$$2 \times 2 \quad + \quad 3 \times 2 \quad = 10 \text{ pegs}$$

There are eleven mittens.
There are five pairs and one odd one.
The other one must have been dropped.

$$2 \times 5 + 1 = 11$$
$$11 + 1 = 12 \text{ or } 12 - 1 = 11$$

The Green Window
The Faraway Tree
Monday morning

Dear Children,
   Have you heard lots of water swishing down our tree lately? I wouldn't
be surprised. Dame Washalot has been very, very busy. She does most
of the washing for the elves and pixies in the woods, but as it has been
raining so much she just can't get it all dry. She has run out of space
on the branches where she pegs out the clothes. Do you have any space
in your room where she could hang some washing? She has so many
socks as the pixies keep trying to jump across all the puddles...and you
can guess what happens can't you!!
I hope you can help us,
Silky

Much of the discovery of mathematical processes within this theme
came from the growing awareness of pattern. The children became
more and more interested in, and surprised at, the number of patterns
they could find in everyday items such as Silky's vase of flowers.

The children created a secret path to the Faraway Tree — a strip
of clear plastic. Along the path they made patterns. These could be
continued by others, or copied, depending on the particular pattern

and instructions. They wrote short problem-solving activities which needed to be completed before you could continue along the path. I found this ideal for extension and special assistance activities.

One day Dame Washalot hung her clothes line right across the middle of our yard. First of all she hung two pairs of socks on the left hand side. One pair of socks had round pegs, and the other straight pegs.

Next she hung a small pair of mittens at the right hand end of the line. One mitten had its cord dangling down.

Up above the mittens in the top right hand corner were four large leaves. Hiding in them was a bird — we could only see his beak. That silly bird — he thought the mitten cord was a long worm. He had it in his beak, but was wondering why it didn't taste very nice! Creeping along from the middle of the clothes line was a fat, juicy caterpillar. When it came to the mittens it walked up along the cord. Where did it end?

Dame Washalot went back for the rest of the clothes. She put her clothes basket down on the grass under the middle of the line. She had lots of washing piled up.

The Saucepan Man went to help her. He hung a long scarf lengthwise along the line.

'Oh no, Saucepan Man. It takes up too much room. Fold it in half and let it hang vertically from the line. That's better.'

Then Dame Washalot hung out two of Silky's dresses to the left of the scarf, and a jumper on the right. Between the jumper and mittens she just fitted in a teatowel.

But poor Dame Washalot! She didn't know there was a mischievous cockatoo watching from up the top of the gum tree. He loved snapping things with his strong beak.

He started at the left of the line and walking along broke off the first, fourth and tenth pegs, then the last three.

Which clothes would stay on the line?

Which clothes would drop onto the ground?

What might happen to the second-last mitten?

As this story was told to the children they drew it on their individual chalkboards. The boards allowed for easy correction and on-going change, which paper and pens would not.

A number of similar stories assisted in the development of spatial relations, ordinal and cardinal number and mathematical computation.

Often the children would contribute to the story as it progressed. From a picture they could also give their partner a description and see if the picture turned out the same. They not only had to interpret instructions but be able to provide their own.

A group of competent eight and nine year olds had a habit of quickly reading a problem and making the 'appropriate' calculations. They needed experience in thinking through their problems. They didn't always stop to think what they were answering. They often visited our tree, so their teacher set them their own 'Dame Slap maths'.

After the initial surprise of discovering they hadn't solved the problem — just added and subtracted numbers — they delightedly brought the problems to us. Nonsense, but it showed the children the necessity of 'thinking through' the task and the required answer before beginning building, counting and further computations.

Dame Slap Maths

1 Silky had three cats, Moonface had six dogs, Saucepan Man had twenty whistles and Mr Watzisname had nine horses. How many animals did they have between them?

2 Jo had twenty-three chickens with green wings and Bessie had nineteen elephants with blue ears. Fourteen chickens ran away. How many chickens were left?

3 Moonface made six Pop Biscuits and ten Shock Toffees. Suddenly the Shock Toffees doubled and there were twice as many. How many Pop Biscuits did he have?

4 Dame Washalot did six loads of washing in one hour. She slept every second day. How many loads of washing would she do in three hours?

5 Fanny had nine mice, Bessie had six mice and Jo had five mice. How many cats could the Saucepan Man find?

This unit lasted eight weeks. At no time did the children's interest wain. However not all activities would need to be attempted and the time spent on each would vary from group to group.

You will probably find, when trying one of these activities, that your children's interests and needs may lead you in a new direction. Any of these activities could have been followed in a number of directions, and varied to suit different age groups. These were what I chose and led the children to choose to enable and ensure development in the areas I had determined they needed.

Party Time

Birthdays

Is there ever a child who remains inattentive or uninterested when he or she hears the word 'birthday'? I doubt it. I certainly listen.

At the beginning of the school year, when I first hear, or am told, 'It's my birthday soon', we look at our calendar. With school records in hand, the children and I write down our birthdays.

First, we determine the months of the year. Which is first, second, third, etc? Are they always in the same order? Check several calendars with children who are unsure. Older children can benefit from a financial-year diary being in the collection to peruse.

Why do many calendars have the previous and following years' calendars in small print inside the covers? Some calendars have the previous and following months' calendars printed on each monthly page.

Having individually recorded our birthdays, I usually find the children are interested to study calendars in the following weeks and then refer to them as needed throughout the year.

Asking the children, then using the class attendance roll to check the dates — especially with young children — we see whose birthday is in each month. Due to space restriction this is usually recorded in numerals, e.g. 21-8-80.

This highlights the need to know the sequence of months and provides lots of reinforcement as you check. Given more than one child's birthday in any month, we decide whose will need to be recorded first, second and so on.

This activity can be a sequential build-up of birthdays, or alternatively the children can write their birthdays on a card, then as a class activity sort themselves into months, then order the dates. This will depend on the age and ability of the children. There is usually a wide difference with young children between those who know the order of the months and their birthdate and those who don't.

Using this chart, the children are able to quickly determine which month has the least, and which month has the most, birthdays. Are some months the same?

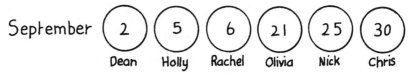

September 2 5 6 21 25 30
Dean Holly Rachel Olivia Nick Chris

Looking at the chart we decided September would be the best month. I asked the children, 'Will we be able to eat that many cakes during September, or will we have too many at once?' The children referred quickly to the numbers and made the following observations:

'They are all on different days.'

'Holly's is the fifth and Rachel's is the next day. It'll be longer until Olivia's birthday.'

'There's Dean's birthday, then three days and it's Holly's. Then the next day Rachel's, then fifteen days till Olivia's, then four, then five.'

'There's three boys and three girls having birthdays. Chris's birthday is the last day.'

'Can we all bring a cake to school on the day of our birthday?'

'Yes.'

'Are you sure? Which day will you bring yours?'

The children sought answers for why I didn't seem certain and came up with numerous possibilities.

- It could be a Saturday or a Sunday so they would need to choose another day, usually a Monday or Friday.
- Their mother might be working and so prefer to bake on a different day.
- They might have to wait until pay day.
- If it was the same day as someone else's birthday, they might change.
- It could be the holidays.
- They might be away ill or shopping.
- One child said he might eat the lot on the way to school. Some children challenged that he wouldn't have time as he lives close to the school. How long does it take to eat a party cake?
- Looking at September, Dean's birthday falls on a Saturday. He could choose the Friday or Monday. As Holly's and Rachel's birthdays were on the following Tuesday and Wednesday, the children debated when Dean should ask for his cake. We put it to the vote and Friday was

chosen. They felt three birthdays in a row was too much! Chris's birthday also fell on a Saturday.

The discussion of the month of September led to the children using the calendar to see which day their birthday was on, recording this in graph form and seeing who needed to bring their cake on a different day.

In turn this led to observing school holidays, public holidays, etc. What should these children do? The children could also find which day their birthday was on last year and next year. Older children could continue to see how often leap year occurred.

What maths can you find on a cake?

When the birthday treat arrives we have immediate interest and lots of fun. We always count the candles and see they are blown out.

Wh! 3 out wh! 2 out! wh! 3 all out!

$$8 - 3 - 2 - 3 = 0$$

or $3 + 2 + 3 = 8$ all blown out!

How have the cake/s been decorated?

The children love this activity because there are so many aspects to discover and discuss.

1 The shape and size of the cake/s.

2 The decorations on large cakes: around the edge, all over, positional, colour or shape pattern.

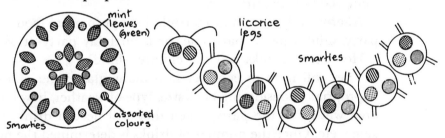

3 The decorations on small cakes. How many Smarties on each cake? How many cakes with red Smarties, or pink icing?

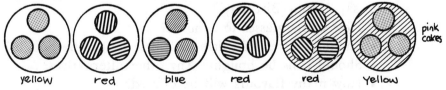

2 with 3 yellow   3 with 3 red   1 with 3 blue

$2 \times 3 = 6$ $3 \times 3 = 9$ $1 \times 3 = 3$

$6 + 9 + 3 = 6 \times 3 = 18$

4 Which cake is the highest, roundest, flattest?

5 Have we enough cakes?

6 What shall we do with the left-over cakes?

7 How many Smarties, if 26 cakes needed 5 each?

Despite many birthdays the children never lose their enthusiasm for 'Birthday maths'. While many questions are repeated and therefore reinforcing concepts, there are always new questions asked.

We record some of the concepts we have discussed and the children take home their 'Birthday maths'.

Quite often they make up a story to accompany this. When the caterpillar cake came to school the story told how the mixture felt being beaten, put in the oven, decorated and turning into a caterpillar. He looked lovely, everyone thought so...so they cut him up! He was glad his smiling face was kept for the 'birthday boy'.

The parental participation is wonderful. Usually the parents let their children choose how they want to decorate their cakes.

Planning a party

Planning a birthday party is an excellent activity — especially if it can be organised to happen. The children can later be involved with their parents in planning their own birthday parties as well. This planning could equally apply to a Christmas party, Year 6 graduation, etc.

The children can list all the types of food you can buy for a party. This can be classified into savoury foods, cakes, sweets, and a balance sought. If all types of food are listed the children could select different menus. They would need to consider variety of flavour, taste, presentation, cooking required, etc.

Alternatively, the children could list appropriate foods for a child's party, adult's party, barbecue, or a birthday party at McDonald's.

How many drinks will the children have?

They will need to consider how many glasses per child would be appropriate, considering glass size, type of weather, how long the children will be at the party, when they will need a drink, e.g. after a game, etc. Once the number of drinks is determined the number and size of bottles or cans can be found. (The children should consider parents having a drink, one being spilt or someone extra calling in to say 'Happy Birthday'.)

How many glasses to a bottle?

- Should 1 litre, 1.25 litre or 2 litre bottles be bought?
- Should cans be bought? Any other alternatives?
- How many flavours will be offered?
- Do we buy three 2 litre bottles of Coke or should we have six 1.25 litre bottles in six flavours?

The children might like to survey and graph the results of people's favourite flavours. Should they only buy the favourite flavour? Looking at the most popular, in what proportion to each other should they be bought?

Use local supermarket advertising. Many supermarkets will gladly supply a small quantity of useful material and they regularly have circulars advertising their weekly specials. Daily newspapers carry major supermarket advertisements, too. The children can look through these to find suitable party food, ascertain how much it will cost, compare prices from supermarket to supermarket, and find which is the best value and why. While an item may be cheaper on special, if you will not use that amount, it may not prove to be 'cheaper' after all.

How many, or how much, will be needed?

How many people will be there?

Will they have one of each of three different doughnuts or all have three from a choice of six?

An endless possible combination of doughnuts could be made.

Will have to buy in fours – so three of each not possible.

There are eight children coming to my party. Mum said I can have a Doughnut Party! We can have three different ones each.
The Safeway catalogue shows six different sorts – iced, jam, cinnamon, cream, frog shapes and long ones.
They sell them in packets of four that are all the same.
How many packets will I need?
Which types will I choose?

Children need to consider and decide if parents, sisters, pets, etc, will be eating.

Children list different types from catalogue.

Determine that the doughnuts in each packet are the same from the catalogue photograph.

As the children compile their shopping list you may like them to act out how they would make the food, e.g. the cakes. They will realise the need for butter, flour, icing sugar, cream, sauce, etc.

What other items do we buy for a party?

Many party purchases are sold in packets. Children will need to consider this in their list of purchases, especially if they are seeking particular colours, e.g. green and red party hats.

- Do all packets have the same combinations of colours?
- Can you buy the items individually? Compare newsagent supplies to department stores.

This activity will be even more meaningful if the children go to the shops or telephone to make their enquiries. They many need to consider alternatives to their first choice before they shop.

Lots of short problem-solving activities could be listed following the excursion to the shops or the data collection.

Claire has invited six friends to her party. and this afternoon she is helping her mum with the shopping. Her older brother Jason is coming to help, too.

Her mum said they would need at least four cocktail frankfurts each and two party pies and one sausage roll each.

How many packets of each should Claire get? — there are 14 cocktail frankfurts in a packet. How many sausage rolls and pies are in a packet? Will there be any left over for Dad's supper?

The children will need to consider:
- How many will be at the party?
- Will Dad be home?
- Will Mum and Dad eat?
- Will grandparents be there?
- How many sausage rolls and pies to a packet?
- Is there an alternative way to buy them?

Foil and plastic pie plates are a great aid during this activity, used to simulate pies.

When all the party food is organised you might like to try setting the table.
- Will you have enough chairs?
- Where will you place them?
- Do you want name tags?
- How many plates, glasses, knives and forks, serviettes, toothpicks, straws do you need?
- Where will you place them?
- Will they all be on the table at once?

I had overheard Kristy and her mum providing directions on how to reach their house for her party after school.

I gave the children the map and story opposite for their language and mathematics that day.

The children enjoyed planning the routes to be taken before arriving at McDonald's. They also posed further questions such as 'Did Tony and Alex go straight to the party or home first to change, after swimming?'

Pet Shop	Delicates	ARCADE	Sports / Dress / Newsagent	Bank
Toy Shop	Cake Shop		Supermarket	Park / McDonalds

Alex	Belinda	Michael
Maria	Brett	Claire

Leisure Centre

Ashley	Andrew	Kristy	Tony	Kate
School		Kinder	Paddock	

It's Kristy's birthday today and her birthday party is after school at McDonald's. It is going to be such a busy day!

This morning her mum is driving her to school, then when she has taken her sister Rachel to kindergarten she is going to the supermarket to buy some more soft drink. (We drank some when visitors came last night.) Then she must remember to buy the birthday cake and to buy eight pink candles. When she has been to collect Rachel from kindergarten she has to call in to see Kate's mum.

At 3.30 pm she will pick up Kristy, Belinda and Maria from school. They are going to change into their party clothes then go to McDonald's at 6 o'clock.

Tony and Alex will have to hurry home. They both have a swimming lesson at the Leisure Centre before they go to McDonald's. Tony's mum is going to drive them.

Andrew's mum is going to drive the other children to the party. On the way she is going to stop at the shops as they have a super surprise to buy for Kristy from the toyshop. They'll want a birthday card, too!

You might like to:
- build the streets and houses and use miniature cars and figures
- make a large chart
- have individual sheets available.

Once started, the children will enjoy selecting who goes with whom and the route they will need to travel. Initially they may need to be directed to solve the problems step by step, that is, sort the information given.

The children can later add their own interpretations. Some of them could go shopping after school for a present. Where would they go for a doll, a tennis racquet, a game of Monopoly, a budgerigar?

What will you buy for a present?

How much can you afford?

Give the children an amount of money, a toy catalogue and see what happens.

The process of ordering and paying for their hamburgers, fries, drinks, etc. is yet another activity. For this you would need a current price list and ideally lots of plastic money.

TRAFFIC

What is traffic?

Traffic of all types is constantly flowing around us and much of the time we are a part of the actual traffic flow.

It is part of our immediate environment, often influencing our actions, and is a theme relevant to children and adults at most times.

We started our study as an overall awareness programme of the importance of bikes, cars, trucks, trains, trams and buses; their similarities and differences and, most importantly, road safety awareness.

Most teachers found they had an attentive audience — and very quickly participants — playing with several toy cars. Age differences disappeared and a range of models attracted girls and boys alike.

In younger grades we engaged in sorting, classifying and counting activities.

How many wheels on six cars?

$4 + 4 + 4 + 4 + 4 + 4 =$
$3 \times 4 = 12$ and $3 \times 4 = 12, = 24$
$6 \times 4 = 24$ (six cars with four wheels)
$4 \times 6 = 24$ (four wheels on six cars)

When Michael said '30' I presumed an error in his calculation, but he explained that in his answer he had included the steering wheels.

6 times $(4 + 1)$

Parking problems

Positional activities and spatial relation activities then became a focus.

```
Where are the cars parked?
The bonnet of the white car is closest to the boot of the red car.
The blue car has a car between it and the white car.
The yellow car is furthest from the red car.
```

At this stage I had difficulty providing sufficient coloured cars for the activities that were coming forward. This was easily solved when the children made their own cars using Lego and some very racy models using plastic spring pegs as the body and adding wheels, etc.

```
The red car is third in line.
The green car is behind the white car.
The blue car is beside the green.
The yellow car is further forward than the green.
```

This second example has numerous possible answers and will also give the children experience in position work.

Possible answers:

G	W	R		B	R			R
B	Y			G	W		B	Y
					Y		G	W

Which direction are these cars facing?

Many of the children went on to create their own parking problems. The problems became quite involved and required careful consideration of the clues or instructions when being recorded. Children at all levels of the primary school benefit from, and enjoy, these problems.

The question, 'Where are the cars parked?' can easily be extended by assuming that the cars are in a car park. Nominate the exit position and by placing walls or obstacles in the way, see how many cars will need to be moved to allow a particular car to be driven out.

Using manipulative equipment, the children designed car park facilities for shopping centres, high rise car parks, etc. to gain the maximum number of parking spaces available. The older children were also challenged to create thoroughfares, entrances and exits to gain maximum traffic flow.

Older children are not only quite capable of solving these more difficult and involved problems, but of creating them. They love to see you 'stuck' on their problem and it provides assessment opportunities for you. Assessment is a two-way exchange. While you are assessing the children, they will be assessing you.

What is your car like?

To aid positional, descriptive vocabulary development, the children sat back to back. One child in each pair placed cars on the grid and described their placement to his or her partner. Did they end up in the same places? Sometimes. This activity then extended to using selected pieces of Lego or Sticklebricks to construct a car. It was suited to children of all age levels — we just made the pieces more numerous or difficult to describe.

At a later date the children all had identical Lego pieces. They were given three minutes to build their own car. Then the cars were displayed, and we had a wide variety of models. How were they the same, or different? Which would travel the fastest? Why?

A group of older children went on to explore factors affecting motion: road surface, friction, speed, weather conditions, etc.

How long to stop?

An extremely beneficial activity was the study of the time and distance taken for cars to stop.

A number of children brought bikes to school and we trialled them (in place of cars) in different areas of the school.

First we raced to an appointed and clearly marked point, then had to stop in the shortest distance — remembering it is dangerous and costly to crash. The children measured the distances, compared the results and tried to ascertain the reasons for the differences.

'Mario rides faster so he took longer to stop.'

'Rachael has better brakes on her bike.'

'My tyres have a heavier tread. They are different to ride with than racing tyres.'

We were then able to try the same experiment on a rough bitumen area and on grass (both dry and wet).

This activity involved prior discussion, setting of rules and behaviour codes and strict supervision. The learning gained in measurement, time, comparisons, graph and grid work, as well as a startling increase in the awareness of safety, was most marked.

'But I thought I stopped straight away', said Ben, who had found that it had taken him over eight metres to come to a dead stop after a very short, but fast, ride. When we measured the length of driveway entrances to the road, this was even more startling.

What if a pedestrian was on the footpath?

How far back along your drive can you see what's coming? Is the entrance obscured by trees?

What if your brakes failed?

The children simulated roadways and released toy cars at different points. Remote-control cars were excellent for this activity. They had the advantage of continued speed and steering for some studies. However they did not have free rolling speed increases. We provided soft landing buffer zones to protect the cars.

Traffic flow

We studied the number of cars, trucks, buses, etc. that passed our school and that went through the intersection near the school.

When was the peak traffic period and the quietest period? Why?
Would this be the same in the outer suburbs and the inner suburbs?
What time do our parents leave for work, shopping, etc?

The children asked their parents to time their travel to work and to note the distance covered at five and ten minute intervals. As our school is in the outer suburban area and many travelled to the city central area, we discovered distance covered was not always the same given equal time. The children were able to plot their parents' travel on graphs and, more importantly, were able to interpret the graphs and provide explanations for a given point on a graph.

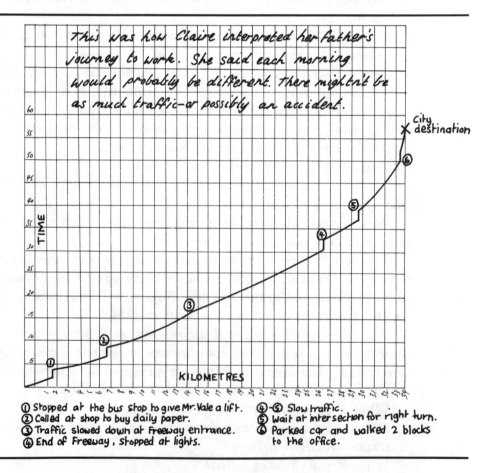

This was how Claire interpreted her father's journey to work. She said each morning would probably be different. There mightn't be as much traffic—or possibly an accident.

① Stopped at the bus stop to give Mr. Vale a lift.
② Called at shop to buy daily paper.
③ Traffic slowed down at Freeway entrance.
④ End of Freeway, stopped at lights.
④-⑤ Slow traffic.
⑤ Wait at intersection for right turn.
⑥ Parked car and walked 2 blocks to the office.

A small group of children timed the changes of the traffic lights at different times of the day.

Right? Left? Which way?

We often assume children know their right from their left as they get older.

My group of five, six and seven year old children made our room into a roadway for this theme. Our work tables were houses, shops, offices, etc. We taped dividing lines on the floor and set up lots of signs: Stop, give way, right turn only, no entry, angle or parallel parking, no parking and parking metres. While making the signs I was able to assess the children's observational and directional skill level.

Obeying signs was mandatory and problem-solving activities such as 'Can you go to Olivia's house first, then turning right into Church Street, get to Ben's?' were posed.

Reading a street directory is confusing for right and left turns, even for adults. Older children should be provided with many experiences of this.

At this stage in the theme we found it difficult to differentiate whether we were studying language, mathematics, social education or health and safety. Our subjects had become really meaningful and appropriate to studying our simulated 'real life' situation.

At the same time we visited the Traffic School to encourage children and to provide them with the opportunity to learn and experience

road safety practices — riding on the correct side of the road, obeying signals and traffic laws — on bicycles in a safe and controlled 'street environment'.

The Road Traffic Authority also provided us with booklets, posters and a Hector Cat Road Safety video.

The Royal Automobile Club provided multiple copies of their monthly publication, *Royalauto*. As well as the children's activity page we used advertisements for cars, car parts, rally maps, etc. in many mathematical activities.

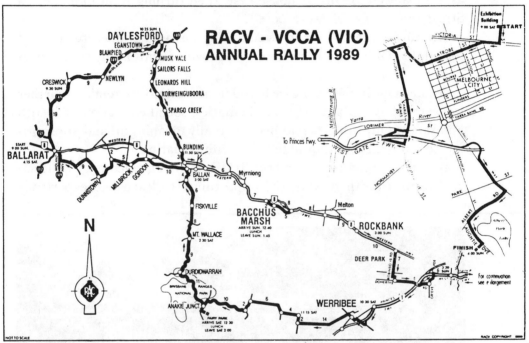

Reproduced with the permission of the Royal Automobile Club of Victoria (RACV) Ltd.

Looking at the auto club map, how far is it from Spargo Creek to Bacchus Marsh?

Is Bacchus Marsh or Ballarat closest to Daylesford?

Which would take the longest time to travel? Why?

The children were able to relate country travelling times to city travelling times during week-end and holiday outings.

CHRISTMAS

All age levels love a Christmas theme, so do include 'Christmas maths' in your activities this year. I have used the following activities with children of all ages, varying the complexity and the length of time taken to best suit the children's level of development.

Decorating the classroom

Paper chains

Everyone makes paper chains. I invite the children to suggest how wide the paper strips should be. How many strips will we get to one square of paper? What measurements and marks are on the guillotine to guide our cutting? How many strips will we need for our chains?

This is a good activity firstly for multiplication, as in the number of squares multiplied by the number of strips, then for estimating the number needed to make the chains.

How long will the chains be?

Determine with the children where you are going to hang the chains. Are they going to form a pattern around the room and across the ceiling?

How low or high can they be hung?

If we measure the length of the room, how much longer will the chain need to be if we want it to loop?

Then enjoy making the chains!

Can we make a colour pattern?

How long will the chains take to paste?

Whose chain is the longest at your table?

Can you join all your table's chains together without affecting the pattern?

The children can complete the patterns as they join, adding more than one strip if necessary. Alternatively, they can leave the pattern, join the chains and at a later date find the changes in the patterns. This is a good activity to encourage observational skills.

Let each group spread their chains out side by side, and in order, from shortest to longest.

Do all twenty-link chains measure the same?

Why or why not?

How long have we taken?

How long did it take to paste each chain in its length? The degree of accuracy you expect in this answer will depend on the age of the children and their knowledge and experience in the area of time. This is how one ten year old child worked it out:

102 chains were made by 4 people

so 25 each and 2 more

We spent 35 minutes pasting

1 minute for each chain + 10 min left

$10 \times 60 = 600$ (knew to convert and how)

$600 \div 35 = 16 + 40$ secs (used calculator to multiply after estimating)

Could have an extra second each

1 min 17 secs and 5

Probably 1 min 16 secs.

Maybe some were a bit faster or slower than others.

Decorating a Christmas tree

A group of six and seven year old children found plenty of maths as they assembled a large commercially bought Christmas tree. First they had to sort and order the sizes of the branches. Each level would hold eight branches.

The children quickly started placing the eight largest at the bottom and so worked upwards, reducing the size of each tier. They realised at the third level that there were still branches left that were longer than those they were adding. There should have been two bottom rows the same size.

'We'll stick them at the top', laughed James.

'What if they were at the top. What would it look like?' I challenged.

'We could make an upside-down tree', said Alex.

'But with the decorations on it might fall over,' replied James. He had obviously thought of the weight of the decorations and whether it would balance.

Could we make it round, or wide one side and thin the other?

The children were so interested in this that we did try one of their suggestions. We discovered why the base was widespread.

Unfortunately, I felt that the tree itself could not stand too much constant restructuring, so I set the children the task of making a tree from triangles. They worked in groups of three and four children and no two groups were allowed to have the same shaped tree. I gave this direction when I saw a less able and confident group copying the group beside them.

There was much sorting, rearranging and combining of shapes to keep the trees lateral. The patterns gradually became more complex after the first two or three groups had completed their tree. The first group later asked to have another try. They wanted a more complex tree.

The group of children who had inspired my earlier direction that no two trees should be the same, needed to change their tree twice as it was too similar to other groups. Finally they completed their tree and it was voted the 'best tree' by the class. Given time, and the challenge, these children were capable of working together and achieving their goal at a higher level.

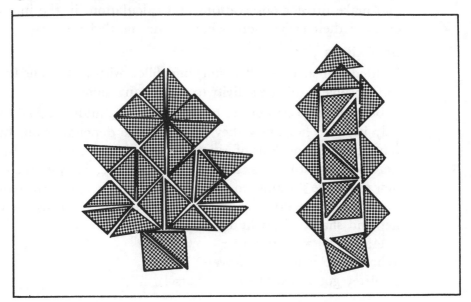

Baubles

I placed several decorations on the tree and asked individual children to place an identical decoration, or with one difference only:

- directly opposite
- directly opposite, one branch above
- on the branch above the highest red bell, etc.

Older children could select a number of the same polygon shapes and see if they could combine them to make a 'spherical type' ornament for the tree. Completely different appearances may be made by folding and joining as opposed to joining sides in an interlocking pattern, e.g. joining hexagonal shapes as in a soccer ball.

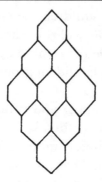
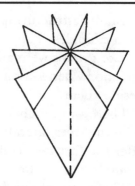

Tinsel

The children kept a record of their estimates of how many metres long the tinsel was. We had three colours — red, green and silver. The children were allowed to change their estimates if they so wished after two days. This gave them time to check the actual length of one metre and make further observations and calculations in the interval. We checked their estimations when we dismantled the tree.

Stockings

I added two small woollen stockings filled with jelly beans to the tree and a problem-solving activity to accompany them.

Being used to estimating by this time, the children asked to see the jelly beans. They knew they varied in size depending on the brand purchased. Their skills of estimating had become very good and they were keen to estimate as accurately as possible. They even considered how much the stocking would stretch with the weight of the jelly beans. We filled up the stocking and started counting. Geoffrey was the winner and shared the jelly beans.

$145 \div 27 = 5$ and 10 r.

What to do with the leftovers?

Geoffrey got to eat them of course!

Christmas presents

We wrapped up parcels (boxes) and placed them on and under the tree.
- What could be in this parcel?
- What shape is in the parcel?
- Place the parcels in order from smallest to largest, lightest to heaviest, roundest to squarest, etc.

You could introduce price tags or department store Christmas catalogues and lead the children to experiences with money. Older children might consider Bankcard facilities. How much extra will they end up paying?

Gift paper

There is such an array of Christmas paper. Young children can match and sort according to colour, shape, texture, motif, size, child or adult design, matt, glossy or transparent finishes.

They can find the similarities in different papers or in the same paper. Often the same motif is repeated with a minor change, e.g. Santa with a different parcel in his hand each time or the same picture in reverse. The children can find the patterns. Positional concepts and counting strategies will be used.

The children can design their own wrapping paper. They can consider size, position, reversals, alternating patterns, colours, etc. You may be able to work with the art teacher and have the children print some of their designs. They might print a Christmas pattern T-shirt.

Let's visit Santa

Having first found out how far it is to the North Pole, the children can help Santa and his helpers plan for Christmas:

1 How to share the toys. Give the numbers and the ages of the children who are to receive toys. Then list which age-groups special presents are for. Who gets what? When setting these problems you can vary the number of children, give presents according to birth-dates — September children receive watches, etc.; give presents to a certain number or weight.

2 How many wheels, lengths of wood, nails, etc. will be needed to make wooden toys.

3 How long it will take to make each toy.

4 How many dolls' dresses (or soft toy shapes) Mrs Santa can cut out from three metres of material. Supply a paper pattern and ask the children to try it. Remember to follow the arrows for fabric grain and fold marks on the pattern.

Alternatively, sort out the patterns for the dolls' clothes that the elves have muddled up. Can the children pin the patterns together?

5 How many metres of wrapping paper will be needed. You can provide two or three objects to wrap, and specify how many of each are to be wrapped.

6 Will Santa have enough adhesive tape and ribbons?

7 Each year Santa has 30 000 watches. If he has 210 000 children, how can he be sure that every child gets a watch at least once?

8 How to share out the lollies for the stockings. Melanie said Santa gave her a box of chocolates when she helped him in his workshop last year. She helped set up lots of problems and enjoyed finding the answers herself. We made lollies from beads, polystyrene and cellophane and experienced lots of sharing and dividing.

9 You could help Santa paint train parts. The number of possible colour combinations, given 2, 3, 4, 5 or even 6 variables, can be explored.

You have red, green and yellow paint. Your train has a carriage, wheels and a funnel. How many different colour combinations can you make?

EXAMPLE

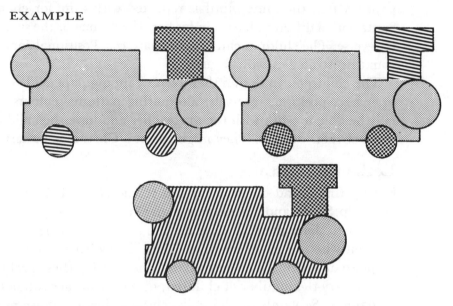

10 How to thread the necklaces or baby rattles.

Santa wrote a letter

Having read the story opposite we wanted to find the plum tree.

Was it the one near the car park or further up toward the back of the oval?

To solve this we stood on the oval in several different positions to see which tree the reindeer would have had to be at to have 'disappeared' from sight. Both trees had plums on the ground which could have been knocked down by the reindeer — or the wind. One had more on the ground than the other. Why?

One tree didn't have plums on the lower branches. (How convenient!)

We enjoyed sharing, weighing and eating the plums that were left.

1 For how many nights could the reindeer eat plums from our trees before they ran out?

2 How many reindeer does Santa have?

3 How many pull a sleigh? (For this we averaged the number of reindeer we found in pictures of Santa and his sleigh.)

4 Why were they practising on the oval? The children suggested:

- To see who was the fastest, ready for Christmas. If we were reindeer who would be our fastest? (We timed ourselves and compared abilities over both short and long distances.)

  Who could stop quickly? Otherwise the reindeer would fall off the roof. This became a good mathematics–physical education lesson.

Hello kids,

When I was taking my reindeer for a practice last night we stopped on your oval for a rest. Suddenly..... three reindeer had disappeared. I was very worried as we had to be back at the North Pole before dawn. It's my special day to think up patterns for the Christmas paper. Guess where I found them. Eating plums down near the fence. Plums are Rudolph's favourite food. He says they help make his nose glow! So the other reindeer want to eat lots too.

Can you eat these? They had too many!! Maybe you could help me decide how much food they can have each week. And how to share it out!

I usually send a big order each fortnight to Safeway.

Bye!
S. C.

- They were looking for ripe plums, so Rudolph's nose would glow all night. It couldn't go dull on Christmas Eve. Plums made it really red and shiny.

  Problem-solving activities concerning time were introduced. Rudolph's nose glows its brightest if:
  (a) he eats six plums every 1½ hours for five days or
  (b) he eats one plum the first day, then doubles the number he eats every day until he eats thirty-two plums in one day.
  Which would be the best for Santa to feed him?

- Each reindeer was practising to help Rudolph in the lead. Maybe they were changing their harnesses on the oval.

  The children decided on six reindeer for this activity and tried to see how many changes would be made for:
  (a) all to have a turn beside Rudolph and
  (b) how many different ways the reindeer could arrange themselves in the harness. We used a different coloured counter to represent each reindeer.

- Maybe they are making a map of where all the plum trees are in our school.

  We made a map of the school and the playground and marked in the plum trees. (They were of the small, flowering plum variety and well known by the children.)

  You could extend this area to incorporate mapping and directional skill development in the immediate and local area. Older children could use co-ordinates and study longitude and latitude as Santa travels around the world. This could incorporate time studies as well.

- Rudolph was practising jumping to the top of the trees.

  The children decided that if he could jump the height of the trees, then he would be able to give a big leap from one rooftop to the next. We tried measuring the height of the trees, comparing them to the height of the buildings which we were able to measure. We decided to leave the jumping to Rudolph. He would certainly need his magic! (You could look at the world high jump record.)

Something special to bake

There are many goodies you and the children can cook at Christmas time. All cooking involves purchasing, weighing, measuring, preparation and cooking times. Biscuit slices need to be cut into equal portions; small biscuits and cakes should be similar sizes when sharing.

How many biscuits should I bake to fill three jars as presents for my friends?

When should I cook them?

Will I have enough time to bake the quantity I need?

A group of six and seven year old children made gingerbread trees and put patterns on the biscuits with icing and silver cachous. We also made different biscuit slices and shared them to take home for Christmas Day.

With a group of eight year old children I made small Christmas cakes. We baked a large fruit cake at school together. We thought of icing and decorating it, but such was the enthusiasm and the wide range of ideas for the decorations, I felt it would be more than worth the effort for all the children to have a small cake.

The children eagerly agreed. They costed all of the ingredients I had used for the large cake and decided on the size they would need. The one cake would cut into four. Then they determined how many cakes, and therefore mixture, we would need.

How much would the cakes cost?

How much would the icing cost?

How much will we each need to pay?

Ideally the children should have made their own cakes to experience measuring, weighing, etc., but due to the restrictions of time and suitability of the oven, I did prepare some at home. The children shared in the baking of the first cakes and then I set them problem-solving activities to discover what had happened as I cooked at home. Each morning they looked for the next instalment.

Here are some of the stories they wrote together.

Today we are making a boiled fruit cake. All of us are going to decorate a Christmas cake. Our families will be surprised...But wouldn't it spoil it if we decorated the cake, then cut it up to take home! We can cut it first and make four little cakes.

If one mixture makes four cakes, how many mixtures will we need to make twenty-six cakes and one for Mr Wenn?

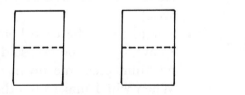

Today we shared our mixture into two long rectangle tins.
We'll cut them in half and have four cakes.

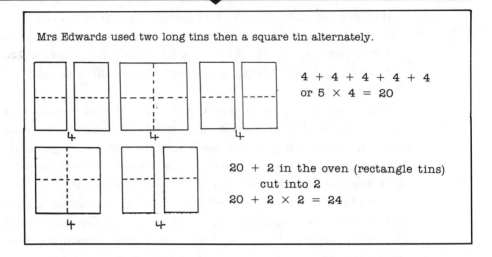

Mrs Edwards used two long tins then a square tin alternately.

4 + 4 + 4 + 4 + 4
or 5 × 4 = 20

20 + 2 in the oven (rectangle tins)
cut into 2
20 + 2 × 2 = 24

We have twenty-four cakes. Not enough! If we make another mixture, that's four more. Then we'll have 24 + 4 = 28. That's two extra. One for Mr Wenn and one for whom? Mrs Deany, Mrs Edwards our busy cook, or Christine our helper?

Icing our cakes was an experience. Very few children had realised the time and precision needed to use rolled icing. We had to consider:
- how much icing we would need
- the size and shape the icing needed to be rolled to, to cover the top *and* the sides of the cake
- how long until the icing dried
- where to best place the decorations
- how many decorations would fit on the cake and still look attractive (We used very small shapes cut out of the icing and painted with food dye.)
- whether the room temperature was suitable for rolling the icing (If it became too hot, the icing tended to stick. If too cold it wouldn't roll properly. This was some children's first experience at reading a thermometer.)
- the length of lace and ribbon to go around the base of the cake
- the best base plate to choose (Some cakes were oblong, others square. We used foil-covered polystyrene meat plates of various shapes and sizes.)
- how to carry the cake home

'I have to walk too far', said Katie. 'I'll take mine home on Tuesday when Mum picks me up in the car.'

'When will I make my other cake?' asked a worried child. I was amazed. I had just finished checking that every child's cake was complete.

'We all have one cake now', I explained, and made sure she knew where her cake was. Why another cake?

'Yes, but it's not quite right. I have Mum and Dad and a brother and two sisters and Alexander only has one sister. I'm going to need more cake than him.'

She was ahead of me. She was already mentally cutting the cake.

'No. That wouldn't be fair to us then', chimed in James. 'We all made one cake because we all paid the same money. You'd have to pay . . . half as much again.'

'OK', she said.

We later discussed how we could adjust the quantities of the ingredients if we wanted to bake a smaller or larger cake. How had the sizes of my tins affected the size of our cakes?

We all certainly enjoyed our Christmas.

SHOW AND TELL

While many themes continue for several days or weeks, the variation depending on the children's interest in the theme and the benefits they are deriving from it, there are other minor thematic aspects of mathematics that will occur spontaneously and concurrently to a major thematic study. These should also be exploited. They should not be discarded because they only have a short-term potential. Many of these experiences are extremely beneficial in reinforcing concepts previously covered or in initiating new thoughts and concepts. Any of these may lead to later, in-depth studies.

The following are mathematical experiences which the children and I have enjoyed and benefited from on a short-term basis.

Clockwork toys

In a class of five to eight year old children I had a clockwork puppy which the children often used during language vocabulary revision activities. One day Katherine brought along her clockwork rooster to show the class. After watching it the children thought they could use it for their word game. Shortly after, concern was expressed as it didn't travel far enough.

'Yes it does', said Katherine. 'It's faster but it's slower.'

What she meant by this was that its feet moved faster than the puppy's, but as it only took very short steps it took longer to reach the finish. When asked to elucidate, her explanation was very relevant and did show an excellent understanding of the movements of both these toys.

We released both the toys together to compare how and where they went. This was initially successful, then confusing. What we could see was not easily recorded.

How best to track their movements?

Placing the toys on a large sheet of paper, the children tried following them by drawing, placing markers, etc. The best we found was pin pricks in the paper, then completing the line later. The children went on to explore:

- why the rooster didn't walk in either a straight line or a circle (his foot was broken, placing him slightly off-balance)
- whether the rooster and puppy always travelled the same path and distance
- who travelled the furthest
- whether they met as they travelled their own paths

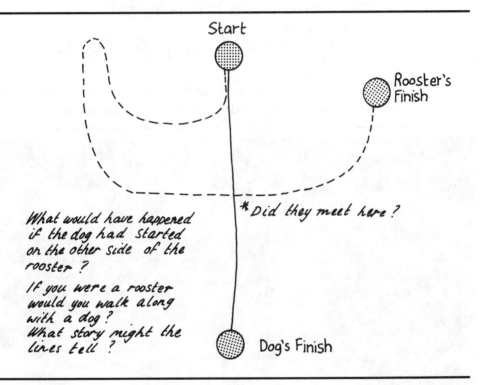

This activity leads easily to the study of chance and probability and can be extended using spinners, dice, etc.

Although it formally lasted one session, the children were often to be found returning to this activity and some brought along other clockwork toys.

Mark brought along his clockwork carrot several weeks later. It walked much faster, but a shorter distance.

This time the children suggested we see how many steps it took on each winding, how far it travelled, and compare the results. They also recorded their results in a variety of ways, providing ready assessment material for me to consider — one-to-one correspondence, measuring skills and technique, counting strategies, value relationships and place value.

New clothes

Jewellery

Claire was proud of the necklace her mother had bought for her 'just because she likes me!'

She showed us that it had a purple, pink, yellow, green and blue heart, then these colours were repeated. Another child pointed out that it had the same colour beads in between and the same number of beads between hearts. This was another counting and patterning activity.

Claire's necklace was one heart, four beads.

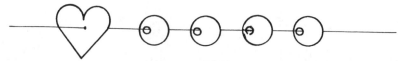

We strung our own necklaces using off-cuts of polystyrene packaging and cardboard circles, and hung them up for all to compare.

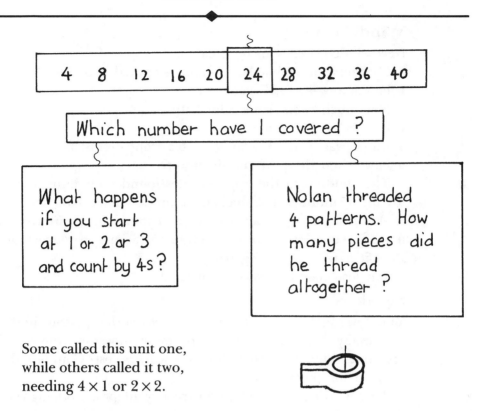

| 4 | 8 | 12 | 16 | 20 | 24 | 28 | 32 | 36 | 40 |

Which number have I covered?

What happens if you start at 1 or 2 or 3 and count by 4s?

Nolan threaded 4 patterns. How many pieces did he thread altogether?

Some called this unit one, while others called it two, needing 4×1 or 2×2.

Some children also incorporated colour, direction and pattern into their 4s threading.

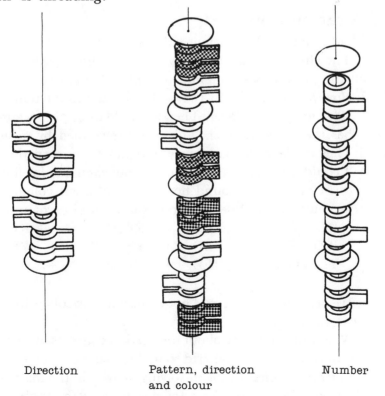

Direction

Pattern, direction and colour

Number

Windcheaters

New windcheaters can be great fun!

Michael's jumper had large numbers printed all over it. We found out:
- how many 4s, 2s, 7s, etc.
- how much each sleeve added up to
- how much his jumper added up to
- which was worth the most — his front or his back
- how much the pink numbers were.

The children in the upper grades found their jumpers added up to a higher number. They had larger jumpers made of the same material!

Windcheaters have a wide range of motifs and patterns. Can you make an equation about the picture or pattern on your windcheater? Does it have a repeating pattern?

You just need a little imagination!

Sneakers

Your new sneakers. Are they the same as another person's in the room? How many pairs are the same? How many shoes? Are the same brands the same style? How much did our sneakers cost? Compare the prices we paid for them.

After a little practice children are very adept at noticing very minor details, e.g. slightly different stitching, laces, webbing not intact, etc. Great for general observation skills!

A rabbit note pad

I had a note pad of various coloured sheets in the shape of a rabbit.

The children asked could they have 'Rabbit maths' and showed me all the possibilities they had instantly thought of.

1 How many rabbits in the pad? Can we count them?
2 How many in one layer? Then we could multiply because each colour has the same number. This was determined by measuring.
3 They all face the same way, but not if we turn them over.
4 'I could use a different coloured note each day for four days.' From this comment we found how many different colour combinations we could make. Older children could combine colour and direction.

RED	+	RED	+	RED	+	RED
RED	+	RED	+	YELLOW	+	YELLOW
YELLOW	+	RED	+	GREEN	+	GREEN

etc.

We also worked on a grid not repeating any colour in any horizontal or vertical line.

What can you notice about the vertical columns in such a grid?

Can you complete the grid so no line has a colour repetition?

I placed another problem-solving activity in the mathematics corner after watching a child let a toy dog bark at the rabbits, one by one.

He wouldn't let the dog bark more than once as the rabbit would have run away.

> Where can you start, and which way will you go if you wish to visit each rabbit only once and finish at the rabbit with the red eye?
> • You cannot hop over a rabbit or circle around a rabbit.
> • Can you visit the rabbits in another way?

In a later maths theme the children tried a similar activity, pretending to visit nine houses.

They also explored counting patterns. They placed the rabbits in 4s and the numeral cards denoting the number at either end of each row. They found the pattern 4, 8, 12, 16, 20, etc., then by starting with one, 1, 5, 9, 13, 17.

Next they placed the rabbits and numeral cards in 2s and explored odd and even numbers. They placed rods to show the rabbits grouped in 5s and placed counters on the numbers 5 10 15 20. They found that instead of keeping with all odd numbers, or all even numbers as for multiples of 2 and 4, they now had the pattern of odd, even. The following day a group of children found the odd and even rule for repetitive adding of 3, 6, 7, 8, 9 and 10.

Meal time

Many activities for all ages can be centred around the dining table.

Have the children set the table for breakfast, lunch or dinner. Give them the menu and tell them how many people will be eating. This can be as instructions or written in story form.

> Guess what! I'm so excited. Auntie Deb is bringing the twins over for lunch on Saturday and Mum says Daniel and Patrick, my friends, can come over too. I think I'll ask if we can have sausages, chips and salad then peaches and ice-cream.

The children will need to establish the exact number of people — will Dad be home? How much cutlery and crockery will be needed?

This activity provides for the development of the addition, subtraction, multiplication and division processes, spatial awareness and positional activities. The children can set each other new problems. The range of food and visitors is endless. Or estimate how many Cornflakes in a packet. It's all fun and it's maths!

Georgia, Christopher and Germaine were setting out the food for breakfast. They were pretending we all went to boarding school and ate breakfast together. This was an adjunct of our School Centenary Year theme.

They asked the other children what they would eat from a choice of Weet-Bix, bacon, eggs, toast with jam or Vegemite and milk or juice.

They counted these quantities and then went on to find out how many packets would need to be ordered for the day. When they had finished, Christopher asked, 'What about the milk for the Weet-Bix?' They had forgotten that. Did they need sugar? How much milk is in one cereal bowl? This was another activity to pursue.

Pets

Guinea pigs

Our baby guinea pigs provided the opportunity for lots of weighing — of them, and of the amount of food eaten. We also discussed their similarities and differences, and their favourite foods. All these activities provided opportunities for recording, using graphs, charts and stories in a meaningful and relevant situation.

With so many guinea pigs we needed a new cage.

- How big would it need to be?
- What shape?
- Could we use our building blocks?

The children used wood off-cuts and blocks to design a cage. Joel worked out a problem-solving activity to accompany his model and asked to display it for the other children to attempt. A number of the upper primary grade children took up the challenge and designed a cage suitable to house the six guinea pigs. These children drew the cage to scale, then contacted the local hardware store and costed their project. They later built the cage with parental assistance.

Joel was building our guinea pigs a new cage. He used six blocks along each side then five across the top and bottom. Each brick needed two nails to keep it secure. Each corner block needed an extra nail.

* How many nails did he need?

* If he hammered each nail four times, how many times did he lift the hammer?

Parrots

How many seeds does a parrot split open in a day? Try counting how many seeds to a spoonful and you will quickly discover the depth and variety of your children's counting strategies. Try different types of seeds. I was amazed at the answer and astonished at the children's concentration and perseverence when they attempted this task.

In how many different orders can our birds sit on the perch?

Again this is an example of possible mathematical combinations.

YELLOW	BLUE	GREEN
GREEN	YELLOW	BLUE
BLUE	GREEN	YELLOW
BLUE	YELLOW	GREEN
GREEN	BLUE	YELLOW
YELLOW	GREEN	BLUE

How do they sit on the perch?

The children related this to their music experiences of high and low notes, then found music to suit the different movements of the birds.

Chickens

If you are incubating chickens you may like to consider colour coding them with food dye or tagging of some description, so you can observe their behaviour easily and keep a record of their progress using charts, graphs, observations, etc. Remember, once you have the charts and graphs, ask questions that lead the children to look for the answers on the graphs, etc.

When do our chickens eat, sleep and exercise?

During this activity the children are fully involved in reading the time, becoming aware of seconds, minutes, hours, night and day, days of the week and so on.

Compare the chickens' behaviour with ours. A child with a baby brother or sister might compare their time spent sleeping to ours. Compare the sleeping times of the children in the grade.

Construction activities

Mathematical concepts are inherent in building. We need to constantly estimate, check and adjust length, width, height, weight, balance, size, quantity, and geometrical concepts, to name just a few.

Each time we add to our construction we are performing a mathematical task, whether it be using simple wooden blocks, or the more complicated materials such as Lego Technic, etc.

I saw the teacher and children in a class of seven and eight year old children spend several weeks working with Mobilo construction materials. They created their own 'Transformer' range of toys then being released onto the market. They studied fit and reversal of shape, pattern, interlocking shapes, correlation of parts, etc. Their studies were inter-related with space travel, time zones, distance, gravity and the concept of infinity.

Rigadoon and the Cabbage Patch Kids

These dolls lend themselves to the study of the number of possible combinations, given a set number of variables. Grouping according to hair alone provides a lot of variety — colour, length, style.

Discussion on the differences between one doll and the next can be almost unending.

Discussing their Rigadoon dolls, Georgia and Olivia even discovered the differences in the stitching widths of their dolls' fingers and toes. They fully explored complementary addition and multiplication with fingers, eyes, hands, toes, ears and freckles.

At Christmas time we helped Santa plan our Cabbage Patch dolls' dresses, given only three different coloured materials to alternate for skirts, frills and jumpers. Later we made combinations of shirt, shorts and shoes — then they could carry either a ball or a skipping rope.

Following a variety of similar activities, older children will have found the pattern in the number of possibilities and can be shown the mathematical theory. They may have already worked it out for themselves!

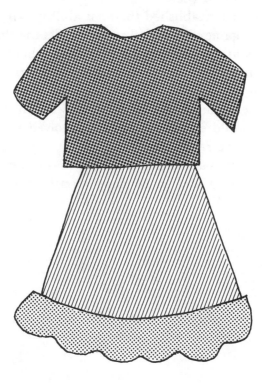

School athletic sports

This area provides an ideal and practical reason for measuring and has the added attraction of being an active, outdoor activity. The children can all participate in running races, long jump, shot put and javelin. They can measure and record their distances or times and graph these for later comparisons on an individual or group level. Older children can determine the difference between a jump from a standing start and and one with a running approach.

Do performances differ from day to day? This question allows for more measuring experience and revision of the skills being developed.

Does the tallest person usually win?

Is height or weight necessarily always a factor?

Compare your times and distances to those of Olympic medallists.

Children are always amazed at the distance a triple jump competitor covers when they actually measure and view the distance.

The Olympic Games and other athletic and sporting activities provide a wealth of mathematical experiences. Try your own heptathlon events and explore the calculations needed to score performances.

Games

Children often bring their games to school, especially if they have only recently received them.

Having first established their suitability, explore the strategies and ideas of the games. If you feel confident, let the children decide whether the games are suitable to be played at school. Once or often?

Time may be an important factor which the children would need to consider.

Does the game require reorganisation of the timetable for the day?

Not all children will be equally involved for the same amount of time or at the same time.

Can you use some of the strategies of the game in making your own game to suit an idea or concept? Can it be extended, simplified or modified?

APPENDIX

CHECKLISTS

These checklists indicate the areas of mathematics experienced by the children during the thematic activities I have described.

When recording on my checklist the short-term mathematical experiences gained, I enter these as a tick ($\checkmark$) to indicate that an area has been covered, but not necessarily in depth. If any particular activity has the potential to be developed further — or needs development — I make a note of this. An overload in one area is also made obvious. Accordingly, I can then plan themes for the future, keeping an even balance of mathematical areas.

The checklist headings were adapted from: *Guidelines in Number: A Framework For A Primary Maths Program*, Ministry of Education, Victoria, 1985 and *Mathematics Curriculum Guide Measurement*, Ministry of Education, Victoria, 1981.

DRAGONS

	COUNTING	PATTERN & ORDER	PLACE VALUE	FRACTIONS	OPERATIONS & COMPUTATION	STRATEGY GAMES
LENGTH	How many scales along his back?	Sequencing dragons. How long to make squares to fit feet patterns?		Comparison of heights	Addition Multiplication Division Scales Ratio of body parts	Can a dragon fit in our room? Where can he turn?
AREA	How many dragon feet in the paddock? Same size boxes.			Takes up ½ space ¼ space etc.		
PERIMETER						
VOLUME	How many spoonfuls drinking choc? How much he drinks		Adding up his food e.g. slices of bread.	Buying food eg ½ fruit bun.		
MONEY	How much is the dragon worth?	Sorting coins Making money dragons Most expensive food.	Using dollars and cents	Make a dragon worth ½ as much 2c is 1/5 of 10c 5c is ½ of 10c	Addition Subtraction Multiplication Division Money dragons	How much is the dragon worth? Given changing values
TIME	How much food eats daily, weekly, etc.				Addition Subtraction Multiplication Division	How long would it take you to eat the dragon's food?
MASS		Who is closest to dragon's weight?		Dividing weekly food into 7 days 1/7 of 53 tomatoes	Weighing potatoes	
VISUAL REPRESEN-TATION	Making scales on dragon.	Sequencing scales. Ordering money		Recording shopping list	Shopping list Making dragon	
SPATIAL RELATIONS	How many feet in the paddock not standing on flowers, etc?	Where shall we place the scales: under, over. Order in size				

ENVIRONMENT — Frog Fun

	COUNTING	PATTERN & ORDER	PLACE VALUE	FRACTIONS	OPERATIONS & COMPUTATION	STRATEGY GAMES
LENGTH	Tallest frogs	Jumps across lilypads		Fibonacci numbers	Addition Multiplication Division Playing leap frog	How many lilypads for 4 jumps?
AREA	How many frogs on a lilypad?	Space 6 fat frogs, 10 small frogs take up etc.		Only have 1/6 of space. How many frogs?	How many frogs in the pond, lilypads on surface?	Nolan's frog story
PERIMETER	Number of frogs around pond	Changing areas of pond		Frogs around edge of pond only needed ½ space	Addition Subtraction Multiplication Division	
VOLUME	Water in pond (tub)	Amount of water for different sized frogs		How much water has been displaced?	Addition Subtraction Multiplication Division	
MONEY						
TIME	How many tadpoles have legs — days & weeks	Which tadpoles are hatching?			Addition Subtraction Leah's frog story	
MASS	Tadpoles	Sequencing tadpoles, frogs		Clay in pond	Adding/ subtracting to pond	
VISUAL REPRESEN-TATION	No. of tadpoles No. of frogs	Differences & similarities of frogs	Nolan's frog problem	How many frogs have green eyes? 3/10	Addition Subtraction Multiplication Division	
SPATIAL RELATIONS	How many frogs are swimming underwater?	Carton frogs in different positions				Placing frogs in and around the pond

ZOO

	COUNTING	PATTERN & ORDER	PLACE VALUE	FRACTIONS	OPERATIONS & COMPUTATION	STRATEGY GAMES
LENGTH	Tall animals short animals Measuring length	Tallest to shortest animal, etc.	Measuring metres, centimetres	½ length of enclosure	All processes	
AREA	Number of animals in cage	Most area or animals per area		Animals to area Sharing food	Area of enclosure — all processes	Where are the animals?
PERIMETER	Number of logs. Actual measurement	Which has the longest fence?		½ way round ⅓ round, etc.	Addition Multiplication Division Subtraction Regular vs Irregular shape	Fencing enclosures
VOLUME	Buckets of water drunk by animals				Addition Subtraction Multiplication	
MONEY	Money to go to zoo	Sequencing Cost of admission Upkeep of animals	Dollars and cents	Sharing money equally Cost of trip ½ fare	All processes	Cost visit to zoo
TIME	Feeding times Travel to zoo	Sequence of feeding times		Time to hibernate, sleep, etc.	All processes	
MASS	Weighing food	Greatest to least amount of food	Weighing grams kilograms	Weighing food. Compare fractions & decimals 1.2 kg food	All processes involving kilograms	
VISUAL REPRESEN-TATION	No. of animals in each enclosure	Animals in classroom zoo			All processes — area of enclosures	
SPATIAL RELATIONS	How many monkeys — in the cage — up the tree	Which enclosure has most space, trees in corner, etc.			Where are animals, fence posts, etc?	Animals in classroom zoo

THE FARAWAY TREE

	COUNTING	PATTERN & ORDER	PLACE VALUE	FRACTIONS	OPERATIONS & COMPUTATION	STRATEGY GAMES
LENGTH	How many socks fit along line? Largest bristle	Which is tallest tree?		Comparison of trees, branches	Addition	
AREA	Number of leaves		Counting leaves No. of bristles in toothbrush		Addition Subtraction Multiplication — toothbrush bristles	How much wire to make the tree?
PERIMETER					Bristles around outside of toothbrush	
VOLUME	Paste in a container				Addition Subtraction	
MONEY					Addition Multiplication How much money from the Tooth Fairy?	
TIME	Days, weeks, fortnight, months	Age of trees Time taken for toffees to melt in mouth, in jar		Woodpeckers help with the toothbrush	Addition Multiplication 8s, 10s No. of bristles	
MASS		Sorting toffees No. of bites in apples		1 apple, 7 bites 1/7 ate ½, ¼	Addition Multiplication — apple bites — size of giant's teeth	Making toffees
VISUAL REPRESEN- TATION	No. of leaves, toffees, bristles etc. Silky's flowers	Ordering bristles Flowers, etc. on tree	Grouping 10s on brush	Giants mouthful of teeth	Addition Multiplication — toothbrush	Where to place Silky's flowers
SPATIAL RELATIONS	Clothes on line — upside down, pairs, etc.	Organising branches on tree		Where to place toothbrush bristles	Pegging out clothes	How big would a saucepan be to fit on your head?

PARTY TIME

	COUNTING	PATTERN & ORDER	PLACE VALUE	FRACTIONS	OPERATIONS & COMPUTATION	STRATEGY GAMES
LENGTH						
AREA	How many to cover the cake?	Setting the table		Cutting up the birthday cake		
PERIMETER	Decorations around cake	Pattern of lollies, etc. on cake		Spacing cuts between decorations	Addition — patterns Subtraction — eating Division — spacing Multiplication — decorations	I have 72 Smarties Where will I place them?
VOLUME	How many cakes will fit in the container to bring to school How it decreases			Sharing mixture into cake tins How many drinks from 1 L bottle	Addition Subtraction Multiplication Division How many drinks for 7ch'n, 3 each	How many bottles of drink do I buy?
MONEY	How much will party food cost?		Using dollars and cents when shopping		Addition Subtraction Multiplication Division	What can I buy? Which is the cheapest?
TIME	No of days or months until birthday. Cardinal & ordinal no.	Sequence of days, months years		Small cakes take ½ as long to cook	Baking time	Time taken to get to party. When to bring cakes to school
MASS		Which cake is the biggest Weighing ingredients			Addition Subtraction Multiplication — weighing ingredients	
VISUAL REPRESEN- TATION	No. of cakes, sweets recorded	Patterns on cakes. Largest to smallest		How we shared our cakes — 1/2s 1/4s 1/10s etc.	Showing what was bought for party food Addition Multiplication	Making a birthday game or travel route
SPATIAL RELATIONS		Where to place candles, dec'ns Placement of table napkins, etc.			Addition Subtraction Multiplication Division	

TRAFFIC

	COUNTING	PATTERN & ORDER	PLACE VALUE	FRACTIONS	OPERATIONS & COMPUTATION	STRATEGY GAMES
LENGTH	How many cars will fit along road	Sequence length of vehicles				
AREA	Number of cars in carpark	Where can the cars park Tyre tread			Car parking problem — all processes	How to plan exits and entrances
PERIMETER	Drive around edge of traffic Edging along road					
VOLUME	Number of cars on road	When is heaviest traffic flow What truck is carrying			Finding average traffic flow	
MONEY						
TIME	How many seconds to stop	Who stopped first, last		Time taken to travel 100 km/60 mins	Addition Subtraction Multiplication Division	Time taken to travel from location to location
MASS						
VISUAL REPRESEN-TATION	Number of cars, bikes etc.	Graphs — time taken to travel			How many wheels on six cars?	Describe travel graphs Road maps Street signs
SPATIAL RELATIONS	Which cars went where?	Colour sequencing of parked cars. Where in carpark?				How are the cars parked? Make a car like mine

CHRISTMAS

	COUNTING	PATTERN & ORDER	PLACE VALUE	FRACTIONS	OPERATIONS & COMPUTATION	STRATEGY GAMES
LENGTH	Number of loops in chain	Chains — longest to shortest. Length of tinsel	Metres & centimetres — cloth, tinsel	Cutting up cake	All processes Ribbons, tinsel, materials, etc.	
AREA	Number of houses on map to visit No. of motifs on sheet of gift paper	Decorations on tree Icing patterns Santa's dolls patterns		Cutting cakes Cutting paper strips ½ girls get dolls	All processes	Mapping plum trees in school area
PERIMETER	Chains around room				Addition Multiplication	
VOLUME	Number of jelly beans in stocking				Rudolph's plums	Number of plums for Santa to feed Rudolph
MONEY	How much to buy presents Make cakes	Most to least expensive present	Dollars and cents	Sharing for presents	All processes Cost of presents, cakes	
TIME	Calendar Days, weeks, hours Time till Xmas	Timetable for Christmas activities. Time to make chains			Addition Subtraction Time till Xmas Cooking cakes	Who Santa delivers to first
MASS	Counting biscuits. No. of plums in 1 kg	Which parcel is heaviest? Weighing plums	Grams, kilograms — plums & cakes	½, ¼ cake mix Sharing plums	All processes — cooking	
VISUAL REPRESEN-TATION	Number of cake decorat'ns Branches on trees	Dress colours for dolls		Sharing Christmas cakes	All processes	Different trains Design your own gift paper
SPATIAL RELATIONS	Finding decorations	Christmas tree triangles Gift paper patterns		Tree Ornaments	Decorations	Reindeer in harness What does the tree look like?

SHOW AND TELL

	COUNTING	PATTERN & ORDER	PLACE VALUE	FRACTIONS	OPERATIONS & COMPUTATION*	STRATEGY GAMES
LENGTH	✓✓	✓✓	Clockwork Toy walk recording Discuss & extend	✓	A ✓✓ S ✓✓ M ✓✓ D	✓
AREA	✓✓	✓		✓	A ✓✓ S ✓✓ M ✓✓ D ✓✓	✓✓
PERIMETER	✓	✓		✓	A ✓✓ S ✓✓ M ✓ D ✓	
VOLUME	✓✓✓	✓✓		✓	A ✓✓ S ✓ M ✓ D ✓	
MONEY	✓✓	✓	✓✓		A ✓ S ✓ M ✓ D	✓
TIME	✓✓	✓✓	✓	✓✓	A ✓✓✓ S ✓✓ M ✓ D ✓✓	
MASS	✓✓	✓✓	✓✓		A ✓ S ✓ M ✓ D ✓	✓
VISUAL REPRESENTATION	✓✓✓✓	✓✓✓✓	✓✓		A ✓✓ S ✓✓ M ✓ D ✓	
SPATIAL RELATIONS	✓✓✓	✓✓✓	✓		A ✓✓ S ✓✓✓ M ✓ D ✓✓	

* A = Addition
S = Subtraction
M = Multiplication
D = Division

REFERENCES

Adler, Irving, *Learning with colour: Mathematics. Exploring the world of numbers and space*, Paul Hamlyn, London, 1967.

Blyton, Enid, *The Enchanted Wood*, Dean and Son Ltd, London, 1971.

Clarke, David, *The Mathematics Curriculum Teaching Program — Assessment Alternatives in Mathematics*, Curriculum Development Centre, Canberra, 1988.

George, Jean, *My Side of the Mountain*, Puffin Books in association with Bodley Head, Harmondsworth, Middlesex, 1978.

Hart, Trish (illustrator), *Young Australian Animals*, Valentine Sands (calendar).

Hutchins, Pat, *The Doorbell Rang*, Puffin, London, 1986.

Morris, Jeanette, *The Pond that Turned into a Puddle*, Lansdowne, Sydney, 1980.

Royalauto, official magazine of the Royal Automobile Club of Victoria Ltd, October 1989.

Schleiger, Noel, 'Random, Regular or Clumped? Classifying areal distributions in nature', in Nerida F. Ellerton (ed.), *Mathematics: Who Needs What?*, Mathematical Association of Victoria, 1986.